A Notebook of Trees

Published in the U.S. by
Stewart, Tabori & Chang
A Company of La Martinière Groupe
115 West 18th Street
New York, NY 10011

Canadian Distribution:
Canadian Manda Group
One Atlantic Avenue, Suite 105
Toronto, Ontario M6K 3E7
Canada

ISBN: 1-58479-319-8

Printed in China

10 9 8 7 6 5 4 3 2 1

First U.S. Printing

A Notebook of Trees

Text By
YVES-MARIE ALLAIN

Illustrations By
GÉRARD MARIÉ

Aubanel

Contents

Foreword 6

Making a Herbarium 8

The Classification of Leaves 12

Simple Leaves 14

Opposite Leaves 16

Montpellier Maple, Acer monspessulanum L. 16

Planetree Maple, Acer pseudoplatanus L. 20

Horse Chestnut, Aesculus hippocastanum L. 24

Catalpa, Catalpa bignonioides Walt., ...28

Olive, Olea europea L. .32

Paulownia , Paulownia tomentosa (Thunb.) Steud. 36

Alternate Leaves 40

Black Alder, Alnus glutinosa (L.) Gaertn. 40

Birch, Betula pubescens Ehrh. 44

Hornbeam, Carpinus betulus L. 48

European Chestnut, Castanea sativa Mill. 52

Mediterranean Hackberry, Celtis australis L. 56

European Beech, Fagus sylvatica L. 60

Laurel, Laurus nobilis L. 64

Sweet Gum, Liquidambar styraciflua L. 68

Tulip Poplar, Liriodendron tulipifera L. 72

White Mulberry, Morus alba L. 76

London Plane, Platanus x acerifolia (Ait.) Willd. 80

Lombardy Poplar, Populus nigra 'Italica' 84

Gray Poplar, Populus x canescens (Ait.) Smith 88

Sweet Cherry, Prunus avium L. 92

St. Lucie Cherry, Prunus mahaleb L. 96

Scarlet Oak, Quercus coccinea Münchh. 100

Holm Oak, Quercus ilex L., ...104

English Oak, Quercus robur L. 108

White Willow, Salix alba L. 112

Mountain Ash, Sorbus torminalis (L.) Crantz 116

Linden, Tilia cordata Mill. 120

English Elm, Ulmus procera Salisb. 124

Compound Leaves 128

Opposite Leaves 130

Box Elder, Acer negundo L. 130

European Ash, Fraxinus excelsior L. 134

Alternate Leaves 138

Mimosa, Albizzia julibrissin Durazz 138

English Walnut, Juglans regia L. 142

Caucasian Wingnut, Pterocarya fraxinifolia (Lam.) Spach. 146

Chinese Scholar Tree, Sophora japonica L. 150

Service Tree, Sorbus domestica L. 154

Other Specimens from Your Walks 158
Authors of Cited Plants 173
Index of Common Names 174
Index of Scientific Names 175
Glossary 176
Bibliography 178

Foreword

Thirty-five pages. Thirty-five trees to choose, from among thousands! A difficult choice, especially since it leads to leaving out this or that species, spoiling so many possibilities of discovery and knowledge.

While I faced this decision, the memory came to me of looking for the right trees to plant in the heath-covered land, sometimes dry, sometimes damp, that my parents came to acquire. I could see my father, in his thirst to know the needs, habits, and spread of various trees, plunging into scholarly works, attentively examining nursery catalogs in search of a few rare species that could grow in his poor soil, covered with gorse bushes and briars and punctuated by a few stunted, lichen-covered pines and oaks.

And then it was planting time, as specimens arrived by train in boxes and were carefully lifted out of their straw packing and strategically planted. After that first contact with the young plants, taking in their different shapes and sizes, their marvelous aromas, we waited. We waited for the arrival of spring, with its surprising bursting of buds, its pushing forth of leaves, followed by the fear of the summer drought. . . . When you are dealing with plants, an entire living world opens up, and you follow the thread of time: seasons, years, the life of every individual plant. And the first contact with plant life is dirt.

But if this memory takes me back a few decades, it still does not resolve the difficult choice of thirty-five entries. I have had to pursue a process of elimination, starting with entire groups, like conifers and palms. Nor does it help to merely stick to deciduous or evergreens broad-leaved trees that can grow in a range of climates—Atlantic, continental, Mediterranean. There are still thousands of possibilities! In the end, I tried to pick a variety of forms, colors, and leaf types, including some trees associated with towns and others with the countryside, some native and some introduced, and a few more obscure, uncommon trees, to instill in the walker-collector who reads this book the pleasure of discovery, and give him a desire to continue his research.

These thirty-five entries, then. The right choice? Some will doubt it when they don't see the locust, the apple, the redbud (or flowering Judas), or the pear. . . . But, in the end, this herbarium's main ambition is to use its "little bundle of leaves" as an introduction to a complex and passionate world: plant life.

YVES-MARIE ALLAIN

Making a Herbarium

First, a few rules to respect and some precautions to take when collecting. The general rule, for trees and shrubs, is to take twigs with a few leaves, small enough to fit in the herbarium. It is also always preferable to collect the flowers or fruits (depending on the season) at the same time. Taking the sample from the tree itself is not always easy and may require various strategies or tools, like a ladder.

The samples should in no way endanger the life or the look of the plant, especially when it is young and thus easily accessible. If, for practical reasons, you prefer to collect samples that have already fallen to the ground, make sure that these do belong to the tree above, then carefully examine the form of the leaves on the tree. It is not hard at all to confuse a small leaf with a leaflet, which is a piece of a more complex leaf!

To make your samples, use well-sharpened secateurs, a knife, or a grafting blade in order to make a clean cut. To transport them, make a simple carrier with two pieces of strong cardboard about twelve by sixteen inches, wrapped with a belt or strong elastic, and filled with absorbent paper. While collecting, place your samples inside between the pages. Though not as good, it is also possible to put your samples in plastic bags, as long as you take them out as soon as possible on returning home. So that you don't forget the information out in the field, be sure to give a number to each sample, then write the same number in a notebook along with the pertinent information in the form of a label (see page 11).

Finally, in most cases it is best to get permission from the owner or owners of the tree, or from the authorities responsible for parks open to the public.

Drying Your Specimens

It is not necessary to separate the various parts of a collected plant, or separate the leaves from the twigs. But in our particular case, and in order to better use our herbarium book, it seems appropriate for the majority of the plant descriptions, to separate an entire leaf from its twig, so that it can easily be placed in one of the pockets in this book. We would also suggest that you make two drying presses, one for flat leaves, the other for stems, flowers, and eventually fruit.

In both cases, the method is similar. Cut two twelve-by-sixteen-inch pieces of plywood that will be used to make a kind of sandwich, one on top of the other, with newspaper or blotting paper in between. On the first board place three or four pieces of absorbent paper, or a piece of cardboard, then the sample you want to dry, with its collecting number and label. Follow this with some more sheets of paper, and so on. Do not dry more than a dozen samples at one time. When all is ready, cover the stack with the second board and place a heavy weight (a few large books, for instance) squarely on top. Keep this quick press somewhere dry and well ventilated. Check all of your samples the next day, and replace any damp paper. Use this time to rearrange any pieces that have creased. This should be repeated several times during the drying period.

The drying is done when the sample is rigid or brittle and no longer feels fresh to the touch. Now it can be transferred to your herbarium. Attach one leaf, perhaps, to the blank page in your herbarium, using instead little pieces of clear, matte tape (this is preferable to using glue). To avoid unsightly finger marks on the tape, discard the first piece, then pull the tape out of the dispenser carefully with philatelist's tongs. The rest of your specimens for that tree (the twig, fruit or seedpods, and so on) can be kept in one of the herbarium's plastic pockets, or even, if they are too thick, in an annex to your herbarium, as described at right.

EXPANDING YOUR HERBARIUM

Enhance your collection by making a custom-made herbarium for larger and/or thicker samples, or even for specimens representing trees that are not among those suggested in this book.

As you expand your collection, organize the specimens by family, then, as their number grows, by genus—all in a herbarium made of cardboard tightly secured by straps. Attach the samples with strips of gummed paper to a sheet of simple, unbleached paper. Glue the label to the bottom right. Then place each species inside a sheet of paper folded in two, or in a folder, also of unbleached paper.

Following the example below, fill out all of the necessary information.

FAMILY

SCIENTIFIC NAME

COMMON NAME

DATE AND PLACE COLLECTED

HABITAT

NAME OF COLLECTOR

PROPERTIES AND USES

Under "habitat" don't forget to mention where you collected the sample—seaside, marsh, forest, or park, for example—and, if possible, the makeup of the soil where it grew—chalky, clay, or sandy.

THE CLASSIFICATION OF LEAVES

LEAF FORM

SIMPLE

COMPOSITE

PALMATE

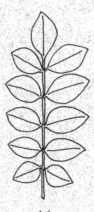

Common Oak

Ash

Chestnut

LEAF ARRANGEMENT

ALTERNATE

OPPOSITE

Wild Cherry

Paulownia

SERATED AND CUT

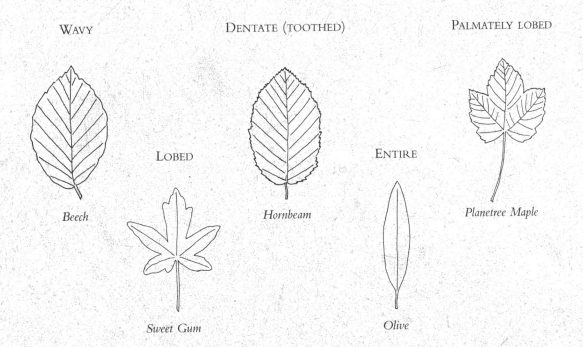

WAVY

DENTATE (TOOTHED)

PALMATELY LOBED

LOBED

ENTIRE

Beech

Hornbeam

Planetree Maple

Sweet Gum

Olive

SCIENTIFIC NAME AND AUTHOR'S NAME

WHY IS IT USEFUL TO FOLLOW THE SCIENTIFIC NAME OF A PLANT WITH THE ABBREVIATION OF THE BOTANIST WHO HAS DESCRIBED AND NAMED IT FOR THE FIRST TIME? QUITE SIMPLY BECAUSE THE "SCIENTIFIC NAME" (GENUS + SPECIES) AND THE "AUTHOR'S NAME" DO NOT CORRESPOND TO A SINGLE DESCRIPTION AND, CONSEQUENTLY, A SINGLE PLANT, ESPECIALLY IF IT IS REPRESENTED BY MILLIONS OF INDIVIDUALS. IF THE SCIENTIFIC NAME OF GENUS AND SPECIES IS FOLLOWED BY A DIFFERENT AUTHOR'S NAME, THEN THAT PLANT IS BOUND TO BE A DIFFERENT PLANT.

ON THE OTHER HAND, IT SOMETIMES HAPPENS THAT TWO AUTHORS HAVE DESCRIBED THE SAME PLANT, AND IT IS THEREFORE KNOWN BY TWO DIFFERENT NAMES. IF THE PLANTS ARE THE SAME AND THE SCIENTIFIC NAMES ARE CONSIDERED AS SYNONYMS, THE RULE IS TO USE THE AUTHOR'S NAME THAT WAS PUBLISHED FIRST.

TREES WITH SIMPLE LEAVES

The leaf is considered simple when it is all one piece and not compounded into leaflets, though its outline and form may be very different from species to species. In every case, no part of the vein may be removed without tearing the leaf.

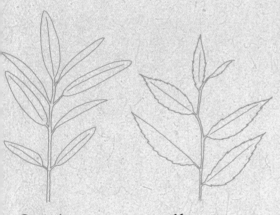

Opposite

Leaves are called opposite when they are positioned two by two, directly opposite one another on the stem.

Alternate

Leaves are called alternate when they are positioned one by one at differing heights along the stem.

MONTPELLIER MAPLE

- Acer monspessulanum L.
- Aceraceae, maple family
- Area of origin: Mediterranean basin
- Habitat: Dry forests

GENERAL INFORMATION ON THE GENUS ACER

Although there are maples with deciduous as well as with semievergreen leaves, it is necessary to divide the genus *Acer* into two groups according to leaf form. The first group is the simple-leafed maple, like the sycamore maple, *Acer pseudoplatanus* L., or the Montpellier maple; the second group has composite leaves, like the box elder, *A. negundo* L. (see box, page 18). Both groups are divided into sections that gather together species with similar characteristics, according to the form of the leaves and the flower clusters: the section *Integrifolia*, for example, groups the decorative Japanese maples with deeply lobed leaves, particularly A. *palmatum* Thunb.

ORIGIN

Identified in the sixteenth century in the warm and stony region of Montpellier, in the south of France, the Montpellier maple, *Acer monspessulanum,* is found throughout the Mediterranean basin and in the Caucasus and Iran. It grows in dry forests, along with the common oak and the St. Lucie cherry, *Prunus mahaleb* L. (see page 96).

DESCRIPTION

The Montpellier maple is of medium size, reaching a height of about thirty feet, and the bark on its trunk is often deeply furrowed. Its branches are dark brown, and its three-lobed, deciduous leaves are small—one and a half to three inches in length—dark green, glossy, leathery, and tough. The leaves fall late, in December, and appear early, in March. Before falling, they take on a gold color. Practically hibernal (that is, blooming in winter), the greenish yellow flowers appear just as the new leaves are opening. The samaras are small, reddish, with overlapping wings.

OTHER SPECIES

The red maple, Acer rubrum *L., a large tree with a rounded compact crown and red flowers, fruit,* leaf stalks, and fall foliage, is found along the East Coast of North America from south Florida up to Newfoundland, giving it the greatest north-south distribution of any East Coast tree species. Its leaves have three shallow, short-pointed lobes, and are a dull green above, whitish and downy below. The sugar maple, *A. saccharum* Marsh., found in the northeastern United States and Canada, has five-lobed leaves and spectacular multicolored fall foliage; its sap is the source of maple syrup, a use colonists learned from Native Americans.

THE LEAVES OF THE MAPLE ARE OPPOSITE, BUT THOSE OF THE BOX ELDER (*ACER NEGUNDO*; SEE PAGE 130) ARE COMPOSITE, WHILE THE MONTPELLIER MAPLE, AS WELL AS THE PLANETREE MAPLE (*A. PSEUDOPLATANUS*; SEE PAGE 20), IS SIMPLE.

THE BRANCH

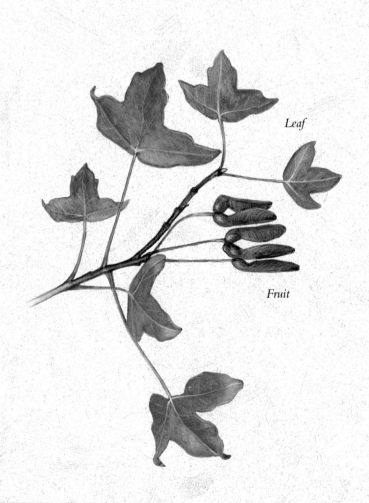

Leaf

Fruit

YOUR MONTPELLIER MAPLE LEAF

PLACE COLLECTED : _____
DATE COLLECTED : _____
COLLECTOR'S NAME : _____
NOTES : _____
_____
_____

Planetree Maple

- Acer pseudoplatanus L.
- Aceraceae, maple family
- Other common names: Mock plane, sycamore maple
- Place of origin: Europe
- Habitat: Forests, parks

Etymology

The maple's genus name comes from the ancient Latin word acer, *meaning "hard, prickly, solid, resistant."* The ancient Greek word for the tree (*sphendamnos*) has the same meaning. Because of the hardness of its wood, the maple was often used to make lances and pikes. The species name, *pseudoplatanus*, "false plane tree," refers to the resemblance of the foliage to that of the sycamore or plane tree; in Europe the mock plane is often called a sycamore. The word *maple* is related to the Old Norse *mopurr*, which described the same tree.

Origin

The genus Acer, *from the Aceraceae family, includes—depending on the author—between 120 and* 150 natural species of trees and shrubs, and without a doubt hundreds more varieties and cultivars. Though extremely numerous, all the species originate from the wooded zones of the temperate part of the Northern Hemisphere between sea level and about 9,000 feet. The prettiest of the ornamental species come from North America, China, and Japan. The planetree maple originated in the mountains of south and east Europe as well as in the Caucasus

Description

The planetree maple often makes up forests with beech and linden trees. It is a large tree reaching 80 to 100, and sometimes as much as 130, feet in height, with a spread of from 50 to 65 feet. The branches are gray and olive green, and the winter buds are green, as opposed to those of the Norway maple, *Acer platanoides*, which are red. The deciduous leaves are entire and five-lobed. Tough, they are a dark matte green above, sometimes a little reddish and covered in a gray down underneath, and become golden yellow in the fall. The flowers are a little hard to see, as they appear after the new leaves, in May or June, in the form of long, drooping, greenish yellow clusters. The fruit are samaras (that is, winged), arranged on the clusters in groups of two. There are dozens of cultivars selected by nurseries for their ornamental leaves; the leaves of the cultivar 'Atropurpureum' are dark green above and violet purple below, and those of 'Brilliantissimum' emerge pale pink at the same time as the new leaves, then become a golden yellow. These trees are frequently found in parks and gardens.

OTHER SPECIES

Another maple often found planted in towns, lining streets or in small groups, is the silver maple, Acer saccharinum, *or its cultivar 'Laciniatum Wieri'. The rapid growth of this tree, which is native to North America, makes it a popular shade tree; however, its brittle branches are easily broken in windstorms, and its abundant fruit produces litter. Sugar can be obtained from its sweetish sap, but the yield is low. The silver maple has large leaves, three to six inches across, with five deep lobes at their extreme points, clear green on top and silver-white below. Their color in the fall varies from luminous yellow to orange and even red.*

THE LEAVES OF THE MAPLE ARE OPPOSITE, BUT THOSE OF THE BOX ELDER (ACER NEGUNDO; SEE PAGE 130) ARE COMPOSITE, WHILE THE MONTPELLIER MAPLE (ACER MONSPESSULANUM L.; SEE PAGE 16), AS WELL AS THE PLANETREE MAPLE ARE SIMPLE.

THE BRANCH

Leaf

Fruit

Your Planetree Maple Leaf

Place collected : _____

Date collected : _____

Collector's name : _____

Notes : _____

_____

Horse Chestnut

- Aesculus hippocastanum L.
- Hippocastanaceae, buckeye family
- Other common names: Buckeye
- Place of origin: Southeastern Europe
- Habitat: Parks, street plantings

ETYMOLOGY

According to Pliny, aesculus, *or* esculus, *was the name for a species of deciduous oak with acorns soft* enough to eat. The name is derived from the Latin *esculentus,* "good to eat," and was given to a tree introduced to western Europe at the end of the sixteenth century, a tree with fruit that is not edible, in spite of a number of ancient attempts to use it for food. Turks reportedly used the seeds to concoct a remedy given to horses suffering from a cough, hence the common and Latin species names.

ORIGINS AND HABITAT

Aesculus, *the buckeye genus, comprises some fifteen to twenty species (depending on whether the* related genus *Pavia* is included) that originate from regions as varied as China or Japan, Central America, and southwestern Europe; six are native to North America. Depending on the species, they can be large, or small and fast growing. They all have deciduous, opposite leaves, a longer petiole, and palmate, composite leaves with an odd number of leaflets (five to nine). Their flowers are spectacular, making up large, colorful panicles, followed by the familiar chestnuts. Horse chestnuts have a preference for cool soil with a neutral pH. They are mostly used as ornamental plantings in parks or as street trees.

The most known and widespread species is *Aesculus hippocastanum,* the horse chestnut. Originating in Macedonia, Albania, and southern Bulgaria, it grows in the humid forests of the mountains, and was introduced to western Europe at the beginning of the sixteenth century.

DESCRIPTION

A large tree, the horse chestnut can reach more than eighty feet in height and sixty-five feet in diameter. Large branches bearing leaf scars (cicatrices) in the shape of horseshoes and thick buds covered with sticky scales are very characteristic of this species. The palmate leaves with five to seven leaflets are large (about eight inches across), and appear very early in spring. The spring flowers are showy, white with red markings, and grouped in panicles eight inches to a foot long. The fruit, which matures from late summer to fall, is a large, spiny or warty capsule that splits into two or three parts, and often contains only a single shiny, brown, poisonous seed.

USE

The horse chestnut was a popular ornamental tree in earlier centuries, planted in rows to line lanes and promenades and as a specimen in parks, but it is neglected today because of its sensitivity to air pollution as well as to summer drought, which is why it loses its red leaves early in August. Its wood is of little value.

AMERICAN TREES FROM THE GENUS *AESCULUS* INCLUDE THE OHIO BUCKEYE, *AESCULUS GLABRA* WILLD. (THE STATE TREE OF OHIO) AND THE RED BUCKEYE, *A. PAVIA* L. THE SEEDS AND YOUNG FOLIAGE OF THE BUCKEYE ARE POISONOUS, AS IS ITS BITTER BARK, WHICH WAS FORMERLY USED AS A HOME REMEDY.

THE BRANCH

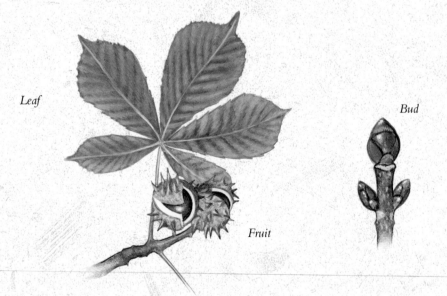

Leaf

Bud

Fruit

Your Horse Chestnut Leaf

Place collected : _____

Date collected : _____

Collector's name : _____

Notes : _____

_____

_____

CATALPA

- Catalpa bignonioides Walt.
- Bignoniaceae, bignonia family
- Other common names: Indian bean, cigar tree, catawba, southern catalpa
- Place of origin: North America
- Habitat: Parks, gardens, avenues

ETYMOLOGY

The first species of the genus Catalpa *was discovered along the banks of rivers in North America at* the beginning of the eighteenth century; it was introduced to England in 1726. The botanists retained a variant of the name given to the tree by the Indians of the Carolinas, *catawba*, as its scientific name.

HISTORY

Since the first discovery of the catalpa, ten other species have been added from North America, the Antilles, and eastern Asia, one of which, the Chinese catalpa, *Catalpa ovata* G. Don, is found 8,200 feet above sea level in China, from where it was introduced in 1849. It is now naturalized from Connecticut to south Ontario, Maryland, and Ohio. All of these trees have rounded tops, large deciduous leaves and simple long petioles, opposite or verticillate (arranged in whorls), in groups of three. The fruits are long, hanging siliquas (podlike capsules that split into two parts), resembling slender string beans.

DESCRIPTION

The most widely known species is Catalpa bignonioides *Walt., with its golden-leaved, bowl-shaped* cultivar 'Aurea'. Reaching fifty feet in height, its top extends out like a vaulted and rounded crown. The leaves, in whorls of three at a node, are very large, in the shape of a heart of four to eight inches in length and about eight inches wide. A light crimson when they first unfold, the leaves take on a clear green color, becoming glabrous on top and more or less downy underneath. One characteristic of the species is the unpleasant odor these leaves emit when bruised. They appear late in the season and drop quickly, without noticeable discoloration. Their flowers are attractive, white speckled with crimson, grouped in large numbers in terminal racemes or panicles at the end of June or the beginning of July. The fruit measures about fourteen inches long by two to three inches in diameter, and remains on the tree for part of the winter. Though not fussy about soil type and very drought tolerant, *C. bignonioides* nevertheless prefers fertile, moist, and calcium-rich soil.

Uses

In Europe, the catalpa is used only as a decorative plant in gardens and in a few public places. In the United States and in China, where it is native, it is valued mostly for the use of its wood in the making of posts and stakes, since it lasts a long time in contact with soil and under water.

In its native habitat, the catalpa is not a diminutive ornamental tree, but some catalpa cultivars, such as the gold-leafed Catalpa Bignonioides 'Aurea', known since 1877, and the ball-shaped C. Binonioides 'Nana', are suitable for small spaces and gardens. A hybrid, C. x Erubescents 'Purpurea', with blackish red-brown new leaves, has been widely known in England since 1885.

The Branch

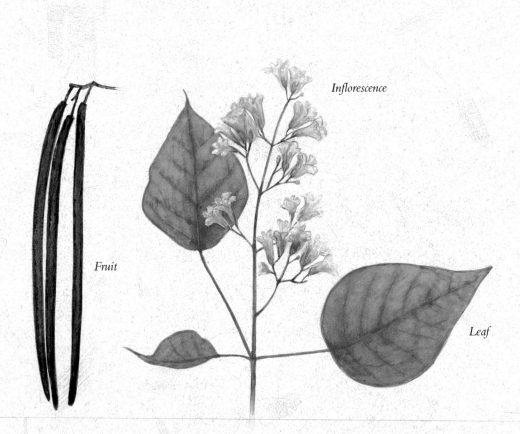

Inflorescence

Fruit

Leaf

Your Catalpa Leaf

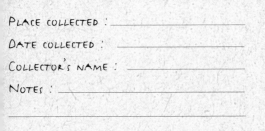

Olive

- Olea europaea L.
- Oleaceae, olive family
- Place of origin: Asia Minor
- Habitat: Orchards, parks

ETYMOLOGY

Linnaeus named the olive genus Olea, *using the Latin word for "olive." This name derives also from* the Greek *elaia.*

ORIGINS AND HISTORY

Though the olive, Olea europaea L., *is a tree well known in the Mediterranean world, the genus* Olea, *of* the olive family, or Oleaceae, is made up of twenty to thirty species, all evergreen, originating from the Middle East as well as Southeast Asia and Polynesia. The majority of the species do not grow in most of North America, as the winter temperatures are too low.

The origins of the olive are not very well known, but it is believed to have come from the region of the Middle East—Palestine, Syria, and along the southern coast of Asia Minor to the feet of the Caucasus. During ancient times, it was planted in many regions and without doubt introduced to continental Greece in the sixteenth century B.C. Its cultivation spread little by little throughout the Mediterranean; the Romans even tried to grow it in England, but without success.

HABITAT

The olive requires ample sunlight and can live many centuries; individual specimens several thousand years old are not rare in southern Italy, Sicily, and Greece. It prefers dry, light, well-draining soil, does not thrive in humid air and moist soil, and is not very resistant to low temperatures; it will not survive temperatures below about 12 degrees Fahrenheit, but needs a certain amount of chilling in the winter to set fruit. Most of North America other than parts of the West Coast, which are Mediterranean in climate, is not suitable for growing olives outdoors.

DESCRIPTION

The olive is a small tree, ranging from thirty to nearly fifty feet in height, slow growing, with elliptical or lanceolate leaves and almost cylindrical stems that are not thorny, in contrast to the Russian olive, or oleaster, which has thorny stems and a bushy habit that rarely exceeds fifteen or twenty feet. The olive's smooth grayish white bark becomes brown and scaly as it ages, and thick and fluted in old trunks. The leaves, opposite and simple, are evergreen, entire, and tough, with a slight curl to the edges; grayish green, punctuated with white on top, they are whitish and scaly underneath. The flowers appear in May and June in small clusters at the base of the leaf stems. They are then replaced by the fruit, the well-known olive, which ripens in October and November. The olive pit holds the seed.

Use

The primary use of the olive is of course the production of olives, yet through the centuries its wood has also been used for heating and joinery, and its leaves used as a remedy against liver troubles and gallstones. But it is due to the production of its fruit that this species has become so widespread; numerous improvements on this fruit have been sought throughout the centuries, resulting in a great diversity of olive cultivars. Raw olives are not edible. They must be treated beforehand by successive washings, then placed in brine. Olives are green or black depending on their maturity when picked, not on the variety of olive. A second important use of the fruit is for its oil.

The Branch

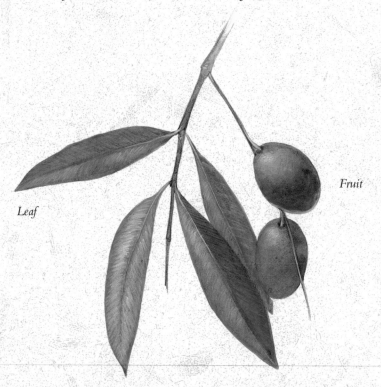

Fruit

Leaf

Your Olive Leaf

Place collected : _____

Date collected : _____

Collector's name : _____

Notes : _____

_____

_____

PAULOWNIA

- Paulownia tomentosa (Thunb.) Steud.
- Bignoniaceae, bignonia family (sometimes placed in Scrophulariaceae, the figwort family)
- Other common names: Princess tree, Empress tree
- Place of origin: China
- Habitat: Parks, gardens

ETYMOLOGY

The Dutch botanist Philipp Franz von Siebold (1796–1866) discovered this new tree during his first long
journey to Japan (1823–29) and sent the seeds to the botanical garden of Leyde, in the
Netherlands. He dedicated the tree to the grand duchess Anna Paulowna (1795–1865), daughter
of Tzar Paul I and wife of William, prince of Orange, who would become king of the
Netherlands in 1840. In 1834 a sapling of *Paulownia tomentosa* was planted in the Jardin des
Plantes in Paris, but only in the second half of the nineteenth century did other species of
paulownia arrive in Europe. Two other notable species include *P. fargesii* Franch., dedicated to
Father Farges, a French missionary in China who sent a specimen to Paris in 1896, and *P. fortunei*
Hance, named after Robert Fortune, a British botanist who made many trips to China, and who
brought this tree back around 1850.

ORIGIN

There are a dozen species of paulownia, all deciduous and originating from China, but some were introduced
long ago to Japan. Although in habit and leaf the paulownia resembles the catalpa, it is sometimes
placed in the figwort family, Scrophulariaceae. It is characterized by its early-blooming, blue-
mauve flowers, in pyramidal panicles, which appear before its leaves. Its fruit is a gray-brown
ligneous capsule that can remain on the tree until spring. Spring frosts can damage the flower
buds of other species in many regions, making *Paulownia tomentosa* the most reliable of the genus
to plant.

DESCRIPTION

The most common species of paulownia for planting in parks and along streets is without contest
Paulownia tomentosa, also known as *P. imperialis* Sieb. & Zucc., or the princess tree. Reaching forty
to fifty feet in height, this loose-crowned tree possesses very large limbs that are somewhat rigid.
The young branches, thick and often hollow, are covered in a grayish brown down. The leaves are
opposite, deciduous, an entire, usually having three or five lobed; they are very large, reaching twenty
inches in length and ten inches in width. Light green and hairy, their reverse is covered in gray felt.
They fall late in fall, but do not change color. Inflorescences, which are formed during the previous
summer, produce flowers arranged in conical panicles eight to twelve inches long in the spring.

USE

A tree that can sprout from its stump, the catalpa is used only as an ornamental, in parks and along grand avenues, in Europe and America. On the other hand, in China, its country of origin, it is planted mostly to protect crops and for its wood, which is used to make crates, chopsticks, and various other utensils and instruments. Soft, lightweight, and whitish, the catalpa's wood is also exported to Japan for use in furniture and sandals.

THE BRANCH

Inflorescence

Leaf

Fruit

Your Paulownia Leaf

Place collected : _____

Date collected : _____

Collector's name : _____

Notes : _____

_____

_____

Black Alder

- Alnus glutinosa (L.) Gaertn.
- Betulaceae, birch family
- Place of origin: Europe
- Habitat: Wetlands, parks

ETYMOLOGY

This tree's genus name comes from the name the Romans gave it. The species name, glutinosa, *means* "gummy" or "gluey," which describes the tree's young twigs and leaves. For the Celts, the alder is linked to violence and fire. The killing of a sacred alder is considered a crime that is punishable by the burning of the "criminal's" house. And since water has no power against "the profound fire that animates the substance of the alder," it was used to make aqueducts and to construct stilts. But it is also a royal tree, since it "bleeds red" when it is cut.

HABITAT

This genus of more than thirty species, of the family Betulaceae, which also includes the birch (Betula), has a considerable area of origin that spreads throughout the temperate Northern Hemisphere, as well as Central America and Peru. In France, four species grow naturally: the black alder (*A. glutinosa* [L.] Gaertn.), the white alder (*A. incana* [L.] Moench.), the Italian alder (*A. cordata* [Loisel.] Desf.), and the European green alder (*A. viridis* [Chaix] DC.). All the *Alnus* species, both trees and bushes, have a special ability to regulate their roots' intake of nitrogen through knotty protruberances. This allows them to survive in poor, gravelly, or very moist soils. They are hardy and robust plants. The black alder was introduced to North America in colonial times for use as a shade and ornamental tree.

DESCRIPTION

Alnus glutinosa, the black alder, has a quite extensive area of distribution, since it covers all of Europe, Siberia, Iran, and North Africa. It is indifferent to climate but requires water to develop and attain a height of thirty to sixty-five feet, often with many trunks. Its leaves are alternate, deciduous, ovate in shape and wide at the end, dark green, and sticky from the moment of their appearance. They often persist long into the season but do not take on any particular fall color. The young branches are greenish brown. The male flowers appear as brownish catkins in March and April, while the female flowers are insignificant. In winter, the cone-shaped fruits, about three-quarters of an inch long, are quite visible. Diverse cultivars and forms exist, some with laciniate leaves. The Italian alder, *Alnus cordata*, with its glossy dark green leaves, is also very decorative.

USES

As a pioneer planting, the common alder colonizes barren sands, potholes, wetlands, and the margins of watercourses. Because of its special ability to regulate nitrogen, in addition to the rapid decomposition of its leaves, it contributes to the improvement and purification of soils, and impedes the growth of herbaceous vegetation. Its wood is used to make packaging and pulp. It has been used as a source of dyes: red from its bark, green from its flowers, and brown from its twigs. The Celtic tribes used red dye extracted from the alder to color the skin of their warriors. It is also a tree much prized for making charcoal.

THE BRANCH

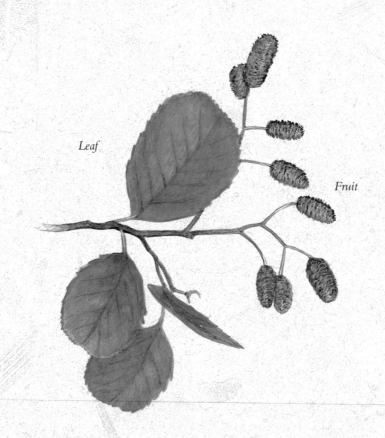

Leaf

Fruit

YOUR BLACK ALDER LEAF

PLACE COLLECTED : _____

DATE COLLECTED : _____

COLLECTOR'S NAME : _____

NOTES : _____

_____

_____

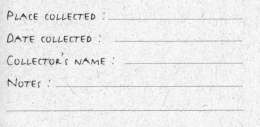

BIRCH

- BETULA PUBESCENS EHRH.
- BETULACEAE, BIRCH FAMILY
- PLACE OF ORIGIN: NORTHERN EUROPE
- HABITAT: FORESTS, PARKS, GARDENS

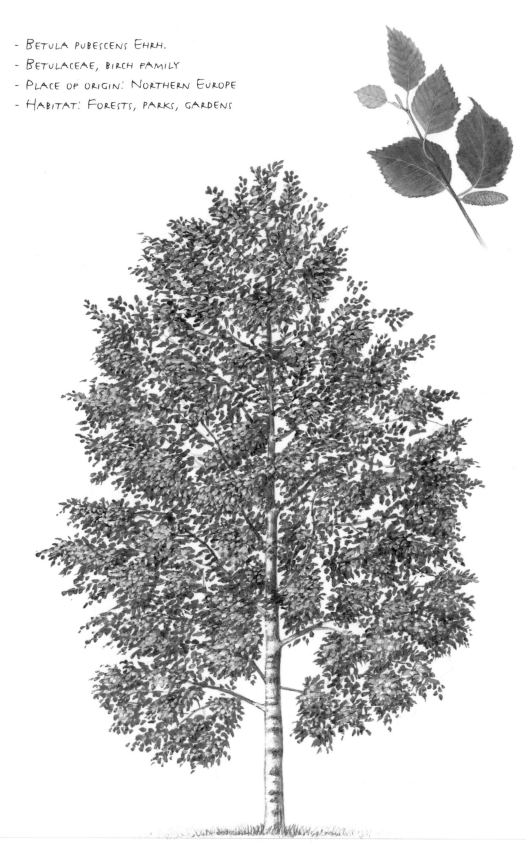

ETYMOLOGY

*Although the birch's name is Latin in form—*betula *or* betulla *in the work of Pliny—it is of Celtic* origin and is related to the Old English word *beorht,* meaning "bright." The birch was the first tree in the Celtic calendar, its branches used by country people in rituals to chase away the spirit of the old year. It is the tree of beginnings because its leaves appear so early, announcing that the time to sow grain has arrived. Birch twigs were also used for the flagellation of petty criminals, and to drive out evil spirits from the insane.

ORIGIN

The birch is a member of the family Betulaceae; the forty or so recorded species originated in the colder and temperate regions of the Northern Hemisphere, mainly in Asia and North America. Indigenous birches are found as far north as the arctic regions and Greenland. Without doubt, of all broad-leafed woody plants, the birch tolerates the most extreme conditions. It is very adaptable; depending on the species, it can grow almost anywhere, whether in poor or dry soil or in peat bogs saturated with water. It ranges in size from a hundred-foot-tall tree (the river birch, *Betula nigra* L., of North America) to a prostrate form less than a foot tall (*B. nana* L. of the European arctic). The birch's limbs and branches are fine, slender, and sometimes weeping. Its trunk is covered in light bark, white or colored, in thin papery layers that detach in fine strips on some species.

DESCRIPTION

It is not always easy to follow the nomenclature of birches. For a very long time, two species that are now distinct, the birch *Betula pubescens* Ehrh. and the European white birch, *B. verrucosa* Ehrh., known sometimes under the name *B. pendula* Roth, were identified under the same name, *Betula alba* L., but their geographical origin differs somewhat, from the north of Europe to Siberia.

The birch needs water, and thus grows primarily in bogs, marshes, or moist soil; it can also grow in shade. Its more or less erect limbs are not as pendulous as those of *B. pendula.* Its leaves are deciduous, alternate, one to two inches long, glabrous at the adult stage, and dark green on both sides. In the fall, they become a beautiful gold color. The male flowers appear in catkins in April before the new leaves unfurl. The female flowers are barely visible. In contrast to those of the alder, the birch's cone-shaped fruits shatter when ripe at the end of August.

USE

American birches like the canoe or paper birch, Betula papyrifera *Marsh., and the river birch,* B. nigra *L.,* or Asian species like the monarch birch, *B. maximowixziana* Reg., and the Chinese *B. albosinensis* Burk., are often especially prized in parks for the beauty of their bark. The wood of *B. papyrifera* is used for specialty products such as ice cream sticks, toothpicks, bobbins, clothespins, spools, broom handles, and toys, as well as for pulpwood. The Native Americans made their canoes from the lightweight bark, as the common name of canoe birch suggests. Souvenirs of birch bark should always be from a fallen log, since stripping bark from living trees leaves permanent ugly black scars.

THE BRANCH

Leaf

Fruit

Your Birch Leaf

HORNBEAM

- Carpinus betulus L.
- Betulaceae, birch family
- Other common names: blue beech, water beech
- Place of origin: Europe
- Habitat: forests, parks, gardens

ETYMOLOGY

Carpinus, *the name the Romans gave to the hornbeam, is in fact of Celtic origin. Composed of* car, *"wood,"* and *pen,* "head," it means "wood suitable for making yokes" for cattle. It is interesting to note that the name the ancient Greeks gave to this tree, dsuguia, derived from the word *dsugos,* "yoke, yoke wood." In English, the common name hornbeam has the same meaning.

ORIGIN

About twenty-five species of hornbeam are distributed over the entire temperate region of the Northern Hemisphere. The American hornbeam, *Carpinus caroliniana* Walt., can be found from Ontario and Minnesota to the north to Florida and Texas to the south. The European hornbeam, *C. betulus,* is a forest tree abundant in the forests of the east and north of France and scattered about the Atlantic regions.

DESCRIPTION

The hornbeam belongs to the birch family, Betulaceae, and all of its species are deciduous trees with simple alternate leaves, ribbed, and toothed. Able to reach eighty feet in height, the hornbeam has a smooth, grayish bark. The leaves are elongated, two to four inches long and one to two inches wide, double dentate, and crinkled with about fifteen undivided veins. In the autumn, they take on a gold color. They are sometimes marcescent and can remain on the tree until spring before falling. The flowers, in catkins, are unisexual and appear in spring, before the new leaves. The fruits, which are grouped in pairs, are small nutlets enclosed by a leaflike, three-pointed bract. In autumn, the fruits are dispersed over time by the wind.

USE

Because of its fine and densely branched habit, the hornbeam was used in the seventeenth century in gardens for the construction of hedges, palisades (large plant screens), topiaries, and covered paths. The decorative weeping ('Pendula') or pyramid ('Fastigiata' and 'Pyramidalis') forms are very often employed in gardens and planted along streets. Independent of its decorative character, the hornbeam, which sprouts easily from its stump, provides excellent wood for burning, and for timber that wears well and endures hard use. A forest of hornbeam is always very clear and open, as the tree's dense shade and root system prevents undergrowth from getting a hold.

THE LEAVES OF THE HORNBEAM ARE SIMILAR TO THOSE OF A FEW OTHER TREES. TO TELL THE LEAF OF A HORNBEAM APART FROM THAT OF AN ELM, SIMPLY TEAR THE LEAF IN TWO DOWN THE CENTRAL VEIN. THE HORNBEAM WILL DIVIDE EASILY AND EQUALLY, BECAUSE ITS SIDES ARE SYMMETRICAL. THE ELM, WHICH IS ASYMMETRICAL, WILL NOT. COMPARED TO THE LEAF OF A BEECH (FAGUS), WHICH IS SMOOTH AND FLAT, THE LEAF OF THE HORNBEAM IS SOMEWHAT CRINKLED.

THE BRANCH

Fruit

Leaf

YOUR HORNBEAM LEAF

PLACE COLLECTED : _____

DATE COLLECTED : _____

COLLECTOR'S NAME : _____

NOTES : _____

_____

_____

European Chestnut

- Castanea sativa Mill.
- Fagaceae, beech family
- Place of origin: Europe
- Habitat: Forests, parks

ETYMOLOGY

The Latin name for chestnut, castanon, *is Greek in origin; it comes from the name of a Greek village* in the province of Magnesia in Asia Minor, Castena, where the first European chestnuts, according to the Romans, originated. The Romans are responsible for its first cultivation in Gaul, and in the Middle Ages it made up large plantations that fed the masses.

ORIGIN

The genus Castanea *is made up of a dozen species originating from the temperate regions of the Northern* Hemisphere, in Europe, North America, and Asia. The European chestnut, *Castanea sativa*, has a very extensive range of origin, from the Caucasus to Portugal and along North Africa.

DESCRIPTION

Like the oak tree (Quercus) *or the elm* (Fagus), *the chestnut is a member of the beech family, Fagaceae.* All the species are very large trees, except for *Castanea seguinii* Dode.w, originally from China, which has a bushlike habit and is less than thirty feet tall. The European chestnut, *Castanea sativa* Mill., can reach a hundred feet in height, has a trunk many yards in diameter, and a top spread of dozens of yards. It is, with the olive (*Olea*) and the yew (*Taxus baccata*), one of the longest-living trees in Europe, living for several centuries. The young branches are brownish-red or olive green with large buds, pointed, and glabrous. The simple, alternate leaves, downy underneath when they first open, are later smooth, glossy, and dark green. Narrowly petiolate, elongated, and dentate, with secondary veins very marked and parallel, they can reach eight inches in length. Although the chestnut is deciduous, the leaves of some species are marcescent. In autumn, they can take on wonderful coloring, ranging from gold to brown. The male flowers are spectacular in the spring; their erect greenish white spikes, about eight inches long, are fragrant. After the very discreet female flowers, the edible fruit appears in its prickly burr, falling from the tree and covering the ground in autumn.

USE

Although it is primarily planted for food—before its replacement by the potato, the chestnut was a significant food source across much of France—its vigor, its habit, and its ability to sprout from the stump make the European chestnut equally valuable as a source of good wood for fires, construction, and woodworking. The American chestnut, *Castanea dentata*, formerly covered large areas of the eastern United States, but it has been nearly exterminated by the chestnut bark disease or blight, which was introduced from Asia in the late 1800s. The breeding of chestnuts for blight resistance, both as forest trees and nuts, is receiving much attention from federal and other agencies, and enough progress has been made to indicate that chestnuts again may be grown in the United States in spite of the blight.

IN SOME PARKS, ONE CAN FIND THE YELLOW CHESTNUT OAK (QUERCUS MUEHLENBERGII ENGELM.), THAT APPEARS TO BEAR CHESTNUT LEAVES. HOWEVER, THIS OAK'S LEAVES HAVE A FEW DIFFERENCES, BEING DARK GREEN AND GRAYISH ON TOP AND PUBESCENT UNDERNEATH.

THE BRANCH

Fruit

Leaf

Your European Chestnut Leaf

Place collected : _____

Date collected : _____

Collector's name : _____

Notes : _____

_____

_____

MEDITERRANEAN HACKBERRY

- Celtis australis L.
- Ulmaceae, elm family
- Other common names: Sugarberry, nettle tree, hackberry
- Place of origin: Around the Mediterranean
- Habitat: Parks, sometimes in forests

Etymology

The hackberry's name may be of Greek origin, but it was latinized by Pliny under the form of celthis. It designates a plant, but without a doubt not the tree that presently bears the scientific name of *Celtis.* The common English name comes from "hagberry," meaning "marsh berry," a name used in Scotland for a cherry.

Origin

*Belonging to the Ulmaceae, the family that includes the elm (*Ulmus*), the genus* Celtis *is made up of more* than seventy species, though the vast majority live in the tropics and subtropics. They include small and large trees, deciduous or evergreen. A dozen species are hardy in temperate and Mediterranean climates, like the nettle tree, *Celtis occidentalis* L., a North American native introduced to Europe in 1636, the Japanese hackberry, *C. sinensis* Pers., introduced around 1793, and the Mediterranean hackberry or lote tree of Provence, *Celtis australis* L.

Description

The hackberry of Europe is a large tree that can attain a hundred feet in height. The mature tree develops a wide, rounded crown with many small branches, giving it a majestic habit and soft shade. The alternate leaves are deciduous, asymmetrical at the base, marked by three prominent veins. Two to three inches long and three-quarters to one and one-half inches wide, dentate, and ending in a point, they are a glossy and dark green on top and grayish underneath, with a fine pubescence. The flowers, in May, are greenish, and the fruit at the end of a long peduncle is black when ripe and edible, in September and October. The pulp of these hackberries has a delicate taste. In good conditions, some trees can live for five or six hundred years.

Uses

The hackberry is often planted as an ornamental in parks and sometimes used to line allées or promenades. Its distinctive wood, without sapwood, heavy, resistant, and flexible, is much esteemed for the making of handles for agricultural tools and whips, which require trees to be coppiced with a particular cut. It is also used in joinery and sculpture.

Don't confuse the two similar names Celtis, the hackberry, and Cercis, as in the more widely known redbud or Judas tree, Cercis siliquastrum L., whose pink, red, and sometimes white flowers appear in spring on both the branches and the trunk!

The Branch

Leaf

Your Mediterranean Hackberry Leaf

Place collected : _____

Date collected : _____

Collector's name : _____

Notes : _____

_____

_____

EUROPEAN BEECH

- Fagus sylvatica L.
- Fagaceae, beech family
- Place of origin: Europe
- Habitat: Forests, parks, rows

ETYMOLOGY

The Latin name Fagus *is of Greek origin and comes from the word* phêgos, *which in turn is derived* from the Greek verb *phago*, "I eat." In fact, *phêgos* refers to a holm oak, whose acorns are edible. This species does not exist in Rome, and the name was given to another plant: the beech. The word *fagot*, which also derives from *fagus*, in turn originally referred to a bundle of beech (*fagus*) branches. The words *beech* and *book* come from the same root, because ancient Saxons and Germans wrote on pieces of beech board.

ORIGIN

The genus Fagus, *of the family Fagaceae, is made up of a dozen species originating in the north of the* temperate zones of Europe, China, Japan, and North America. Sensitive to humid air, these species prefer ocean and mountain climates. The European beech is naturalized throughout Europe except for Portugal, and widely planted in North America, while the American beech can be found almost everywhere in the eastern part of North America. The beech is often associated with the oak, and forms massive forests of a very distinctive atmosphere, due to the light created by the undergrowth.

DESCRIPTION

Beech trees usually possess great stature and majestic habit. Reaching sometimes eighty to a hundred feet in height, they can have an equal spread in diameter. The bark of the trunk and branches is silvery gray and, unlike that of most trees, becomes smooth in old age. The young branches are brown-gray and smooth, with long, pointed buds that open quite visibly. The alternate, deciduous leaves are oval, with five to nine pairs of veins and a slightly wavy border; downy at first, the leaves become smooth and glossy above, and hairy along the veins. Though the flowers are insignificant, the fruits, known as beechnuts, have a very characteristic triangular form, but are slightly toxic if consumed in large quantities. The outer covering of the fruit is a prickly bur, which splits into four parts to reveal a pair of shiny, brown beechnuts inside.

The beech's autumn color varies from luminous gold to brownish red. Some forms, like *F. sylvatica purpurea*, possess red leaves in the spring, which turn greenish red in the summer; others, like *F. sylvatica* 'Asplenifolia', have profoundly laciniate leaves.

USE

The hard and brittle wood of beech is not very durable used outside if it is not treated, but makes excellent fuel. It is largely used for white wood furniture and to make toys, household goods, plywood, soil covers, and so on. As an ornamental it graces parks with its spontaneous form and with the various shapes and colors of its leaves, whether planted as an isolated specimen in a lawn, in a group, or to line an allée. The beech tolerates pruning and can form windbreaks and hedges of great size. Some forms, like the "faux de Verzy," the famous twisted beech of Reims, or cultivars such as the weeping beech and purple beech, are suitable for small gardens. The smooth bark of an old beech trunk makes an ideal surface for carving, preserving initials and dates indefinitely.

THE BRANCH

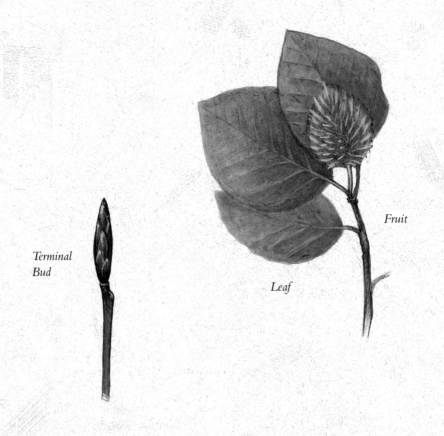

Terminal
Bud

Leaf

Fruit

YOUR BEECH LEAF

PLACE COLLECTED : _____

DATE COLLECTED : _____

COLLECTOR'S NAME : _____

NOTES : _____

_____

_____

LAUREL

- LAURUS NOBILIS L.
- LAURACEAE, LAUREL FAMILY
- OTHER COMMON NAMES: LAUREL, BAY, SWEET BAY
- PLACE OF ORIGIN: SURROUNDING THE MEDITERRANEAN
- HABITAT: FORESTS, PARKS, GARDENS

Etymology

The laurel was born, according to the Greeks, from the metamorphosis of the nymph Daphne to rebuff the advances of Apollo. *Laurus nobilis*, the laurel, was thus consecrated by Apollo and was used as a crown for the winners, or laureates, of games of the academy and poetry. Many universities crown their doctors with the leaves and berries of the laurel, *baccae lauri*, from where, according to some, we get the word *baccalaureate*. In Rome, laurel adorned the heads of vanquishing generals and of emperors. Today the leaves are still used in ornamenting the costumes of various institutes throughout the Western world.

Origin

Of the family Lauraceae, this genus contains only two species, Laurus azorica (Seub.) Franco, *originating* from the Canary Islands and the Azores, and the true laurel, *Laurus nobilis* L., which is found around the Mediterranean. Though these small trees grow without difficulty in warmer zones with mild winters, they do not like the cold, and their leaves are susceptible to frost. Outside of their area of origin, they should be planted in well-drained soil, sheltered from cold winds, or in planters and pots to overwinter in a greenhouse.

Description

Its trunk dividing near the base and branching into a thick top, the true laurel is evergreen and can reach thirty and sometimes even fifty feet in height. Often suckering from the base, the young greenish branches are glabrous, in contrast to those of *Laurus azorica*, which are very tomentose, or hairy. The leaves are simple, alternate, lanceolate, with short petioles; one and one-half to four inches long and one-third to one and one-half inches wide, they are tough, dark green, glossy on top, very matte underneath, and very aromatic due to their volatile oils (containing up to 45 percent of the essential oil cineole). The flowers, which are gold and aromatic, appear in April in the form of small umbels that are not very noticeable. The fruit looks like a small olive, first green, then black and glossy at maturity in October. The berries are rich in essential oils, known for their sedative effect, formerly used in medicine under the name of Fioravanti balm.

USE

Planted in a tub or pot, the laurel can be easily used to decorate gardens in the classical style, as it tolerates pruning and can be trimmed into a number of topiary forms, such as cones and spheres. Its aromatic leaves are the familiar bay leaves, used in sauces, stews, vinegars, and mustards, as well as in perfumery. It is not impossible that, in the search for new molecules to use in medicine today, the old laurel of Apollo will be used anew in pharmacy.

IN THE COMMON VOCABULARY, MANY PLANTS HAVE THE NAME "LAUREL," "BAY," OR THE SCIENTIFIC LAURUS. THE LEAVES, BRANCHES, AND BERRIES OF SOME OF THESE LAURELS ARE TOXIC, EVEN VERY TOXIC IN THE CASE OF THE COMMON OLEANDER, OR ROSEBAY (NERIUM OLEANDER L.).

THE BRANCH

Leaf

Fruit

YOUR LAUREL LEAF

PLACE COLLECTED : _____

DATE COLLECTED : _____

COLLECTOR'S NAME : _____

NOTES : _____

_____

_____

Sweet Gum

- Liquidambar styraciflua L.
- Hamamelidaceae, witch hazel family
- Other common names: Redgum, sapgum
- Place of origin: North America
- Habitat: Parks, gardens

ETYMOLOGY

A French botanist in 1615 described this new tree from North America by using a word of Spanish origin, *liquidambar*, meaning "liquid resin" or "liquid amber" and derived from the Latin word *liquidus* and the Arabic word *ambar*. The American species is named *styraciflua* because it produces storax or styrax, an aromatic balsam important in medicine and perfumery, when its bark is cut.

ORIGIN

Only four species exist in the genus Liquidambar *of the witch hazel family, Hamamelidaceae: the American* sweet gum, found along the East Coast from New England to Florida, *L. styraciflua* L.; the oriental sweet gum, *L. orientalis* Mill., from Asia Minor; and two from China, including the Formosan gum, *L. formosana* Hance. All have alternate, deciduous, palmate-lobed leaves resembling those of the maple. Their flowers are insignificant, but the fruits in October have the shape of a small spiky ball, hanging from the tip of a long, slender peduncle.

DESCRIPTION

The species most commonly planted in gardens and parks is the American sweet gum, Liquidambar styraciflua, introduced in the seventeenth century to Europe. This tree's autumnal foliage has always attracted attention with its spectacular variety of colors and nuances, ranging from deep purple to violet-brown, orange-gold, scarlet, and Bordeaux red. The leaves are five or six inches long, with five to seven lobes, glossy dark green on top, and very matte on the underside. The branches are a ruddy brown and sometimes corky-winged. To ensure the best coloring, the sweet gum should be planted in deep soil, full sunlight, and very humid air. Young, it is sensitive to frost. It can measure up to 140 feet in height in its original habitat, though it is generally a smaller tree in most garden settings.

USES

The sweet gum is often planted in gardens for the beauty of its autumnal foliage, especially in ornamental cultivars such as 'Palo Alto'. Unfortunately, it is slow growing and resents summer drought, preferring deep, moist, and loose soil. It is poorly suited to the dry and polluted air of the urban setting. In a garden, it claims a large space since its roots have a tendency to extend far from the trunk. The fragrant resin styrax, which is important in medicine and perfumery, is nowadays chiefly extracted from the oriental sweet gum, *Liquidambar orientalis*.

AN IMPORTANT TIMBER TREE, SWEET GUM IS SECOND ONLY TO OAKS AS A SOURCE OF HARDWOOD. ITS WOOD IS USED FOR PLYWOOD, PULP, BARRELS, AND BOXES.

THE BRANCH

Leaf

YOUR SWEET GUM LEAF

PLACE COLLECTED : _____

DATE COLLECTED : _____

COLLECTOR'S NAME : _____

NOTES : _____

_____

_____

TULIP POPLAR

- LIRIODENDRON TULIPIFERA L.
- MAGNOLIACEAE, MAGNOLIA FAMILY
- OTHER COMMON NAMES: TULIP TREE, WHITEWOOD
- PLACE OF ORIGIN: NORTH AMERICA
- HABITAT: PARKS, URBAN STREET PLANTINGS

ETYMOLOGY

Liriodendron is made up of two words of Greek origin, leirion, *"lily," and* dendron, *tree," while* tulipifera, of Latin origin, means "having tulips." It is true that the flower more resembles a tulip than a lily.

HISTORY

Only two species of tulip poplar exist, both deciduous but originating from two different continents, quite distant from one another. The Chinese tulip tree, *Liriodendron chinense* (Hemsl.) Sarg., was discovered in 1875 and introduced in Europe at the beginning of the twentieth century. Its American alter ego, *L. tulipifera* L., thrives on rich, moist land and is native to the eastern part of North America; introduced to Europe from Virginia by the earliest colonists, it was already planted in some European parks by the end of the seventeenth century.

DESCRIPTION

Liriodendron tulipifera, *of the family Magnoliaceae, is a very large tree with a long, straight trunk and a* pyramidal crown, capable of reaching 130 to 150 feet in height in North America, although in Europe it rarely grows higher than 100 feet, with a diameter of 50 to 65 feet. The buds, large and flat, grow from the smooth and reddish branches. The alternate leaves, on long petioles, are deciduous. They are almost square in shape, with two large lateral lobes that are easily identifiable. A soft green in color, they take on a magnificent yellow gold in autumn. The tulip starts to flower at about twenty to thirty years of age. Though the flower resembles the tulip in shape, its color varies from sulphur yellow to a goldish green, but is unfortunately often hardly visible, hidden as it is by leaves in May and June. In autumn, the erect fruit has a tapered cone shape, about two and a half or three inches long.

USE

As an ornamental tree, the tulip poplar is above all used in parks and allées because of its majestic habit and the ornamental quality of its leaves. On the other hand, it is sensitive to urban pollution and needs humidity and a good summer to develop. Given moist, deep soil, and sheltered from winds, it can grow quickly. The cultivar 'Aureo-marginata' has leaves margined with yellow.

IN THE NORTH AMERICAN PRIMEVAL FORESTS, TULIP POPLARS GREW TO GREAT HEIGHTS, BUT WERE CUT DOWN BY AMERICAN PIONEERS FOR THEIR VALUABLE SOFT WOOD. KNOWN IN THE TRADE AS POPLAR OR YELLOW POPLAR, THE TULIP POPLAR REMAINS ONE OF THE CHIEF COMMERCIAL HARDWOODS.

THE BRANCH

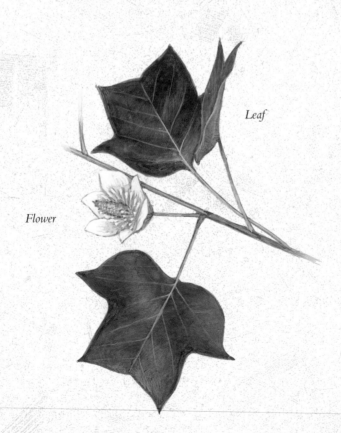

Leaf

Flower

Your Tulip Poplar Leaf

Place collected : _____

Date collected : _____

Collector's name : _____

Notes : _____

_____

WHITE MULBERRY

- Morus alba L.
- Moraceae, mulberry family
- Other common names: Silkworm mulberry,
  Russian mulberry
- Place of origin: China
- Habitat: Plantations, gardens

ETYMOLOGY

The present-day genus name of the mulberry, Morus, *is the same name that was given to this tree* by the Romans. But the origin of the word seems to be much older, and probably comes from a pre-Hellenic language.

ORIGN

There are about ten species of mulberry, originating from the temperate and subtropical regions of the Northern Hemisphere. The most ancient species known is *Morus alba* L., the white mulberry, which comes from China. According to Chinese chronicles, around 2700 B.C. the empress of China, wishing to produce silk, decided to raise silkworm cocoons and to plant mulberries. The "Silk Road" crossing the Asian continent was soon established. Introduced quite soon after in India and Persia, the white mulberry made its appearance in Byzantium in the seventh century A.D. and in Provence at the end of the fifteenth. It was introduced initially to the southeastern United States for the purpose of farming silkworms; the experiment was not successful, but the trees have naturalized enthusiastically throughout the East and the Pacific states.

The black mulberry, *Morus nigra* L., originated in the regions around the Caspian Sea. Known to the Greeks and Romans, it was introduced by the Arabs of North Africa to Spain.

DESCRIPTION

The white mulberry is a small tree with a rounded top, usually about forty feet high but occasionally reaching eighty feet, and with a span of twenty to twenty-five feet. The leaves, alternate and deciduous, are ovoid with lobes of diverse shapes. They can reach eight inches in length and are light green, glossy, and smooth on top, pubescent and slightly rough underneath. They take on a pretty golden-yellow color in the autumn. The flowers, which appear in May and June, are insignificant, but produce edible mulberries.

USES

White mulberries are grown in plantations the world over for the production of silk. Lovers of heat and drought tolerant, they adapt themselves well to urban settings (spreading like weeds in the cities, where their fruit litter the sidewalks). A number of mulberry cultivars, such as the weeping form *Morus alba* 'Pendula', are used in parks and gardens. One species recently introduced from Japan (1918), *Morus kagayamae* Koidz., has very large leaves with deep lobes and does not produce fruit, which is a considerable advantage in public spaces! Although it is of an inferior quality for the production of silk, the black mulberry is cultivated for its fruit, which is used to make wine and syrups to fight mouth ulcers and throat infections.

THE SMALL FRUIT OF THE TEXAS MULBERRY, MORUS MICROPHYLLA BUCKL., WAS A FOOD OF SOUTHWESTERN NATIVE AMERICANS, WHO INTRODUCED IT AT THE BOTTOM OF THE GRAND CANYON, TRANSPLANTING WILD TREES FROM FARTHER SOUTH. THE WOOD OF THE AMERICAN NATIVE RED MULBERRY, MORUS RUBRA L., IS USED LOCALLY FOR FENCEPOSTS, FURNITURE, AND AGRICULTURAL IMPLEMENTS.

THE BRANCH

Leaf

Fruit

YOUR WHITE MULBERRY LEAF

PLACE COLLECTED : _____

DATE COLLECTED : _____

COLLECTOR'S NAME : _____

NOTES : _____

_____

_____

LONDON PLANE

- PLATANUS X ACERIFOLIA (AIT.) WILLD.
- PLATANACEAE, SYCAMORE FAMILY
- OTHER COMMON NAMES: BUTTONWOOD, BUTTONBALL, PLANE, SYCAMORE
- PLACE OF ORIGIN: NATURAL HYBRID
- HABITAT: PARKS, GARDENS, STREET PLANTINGS

Etymology

The Greeks gave this large and majestic tree the name platanos*, or* platanistos *in the work of Homer.* The Latin genus name *Platanus* is of the same origin, derived from the Greek adjective *platys*, "large and flat," which probably refers to the large leaves of the plane tree. The Latin species name *acerifolia* means "maple leaf," and refers to the resemblance of the leaves to those of maples. The word *sycamore* comes from the two Greek words *sukon*, "fig," and *moron*, "mulberry," and is used to describe a number of unrelated trees, including the sycamore fig or Egyptian sycamore, *Ficus sycomorus*.

Origin

Depending on the author, the number of the species of the genus Platanus, *in the family Platanaceae, varies* from five to seven. They all originated in the temperate regions of the Northern Hemisphere. The oriental plane, *Platanus orientalis* L., grows from the southeast of Europe to India, while the American plane, *P. occidentalis* L., can be found from North America to Mexico. All of these species grow naturally near streams and rivers. The most commonly planted species and the one found in parks or in rows along streets in Europe and North America is the London plane, *platanus x acerifolia* (Ait.) Willd. A natural hybridization of *P. orientalis* and *P. occidentalis*, which probably originated in Europe, this species appeared under various names in a number of works on the art of gardens in the seventeenth century.

Description

One of the special features of the London plane is its bark's color, clear brown then golden green to brownish gray; on the trunk and large branches, this bark peels off in large irregular flakes, revealing a range of colors that can lend it a very attractive quality. A rapid grower, it can reach 115 to 130 feet, with a crown span of 65 to 80 feet, with its outer branches slightly drooping. It can live many centuries if it is not regularly pruned. The jagged leaves, which bear a resemblance to grape leaves, appear late in spring and possess three to five more or less triangular lobes of six to ten inches in length. Pale green, they are glabrous above with three marked veins, and downy underneath. The London plane's autumnal color is yellowish green. Its leaves are tough and decompose very slowly.

Uses

The plane tree by nature grows by rivers and waterways; it loves deep soil and the high temperatures of summer. Despite these needs, the plane can grow in a number of situations and is easy to prune; it makes a valuable shade tree, and can be clipped into screens and arbors. The wood of the sycamore or American plane is used for for furniture parts, millwork, flooring, and products such as butcher blocks.

THE LONDON PLANE FRUIT, BRISTLY BROWN BALLS, ARE OFTEN GROUPED TOGETHER IN PENDANTS AT THE END OF A VERY LONG PEDUNCLE; THEY MATURE IN THE FALL AND CAN REMAIN ON THE TREE THROUGHOUT WINTER.

THE BRANCH

Leaf

Fruit

Your London Plane Leaf

PLACE COLLECTED : _____

DATE COLLECTED : _____

COLLECTOR'S NAME : _____

NOTES : _____

_____

_____

Lombardy Poplar

- Populus nigra 'Italica'
- Salicaceae, willow family
- Place of origin: Europe
- Habitat: Plantations, allées

ORIGIN

Of the family Salicaceae, *the poplars originated in the cold and temperate regions of the Northern* Hemisphere, from Europe and North Africa to China, as well as North America. The thirty or so indigenous species and numerous hybrids have been regrouped into five large sections: the white poplars (*Leuce*), the balsam poplars (*Tacamahacca*), the black poplars (*Aegeiros*), and the sections *Leucoides* and *Turanga*. Many varieties are found naturalized across North America. The Lombardy poplar cultivar apparently originated in northern Italy before 1750, and was introduced to the United States, where it is widely planted.

DESCRIPTION

Like all of the black poplars, Populus nigra L., *the fastigiate variety P. nigra 'Italica', the Lombardy poplar,* grows well in fluvial depressions and humid forests in well-drained, sandy, stony, deep, and rich soil that may be periodically soaked or flooded. It is a large tree that grows rapidly on a narrow trunk and fills in as it ages. The Lombardy poplar is also a large tree that can reach 130 feet in an erect column formed by many principal branches that part at the base to rise up to the top of the tree. The lateral branches are also straightt and numerous.

The young branches are yellow-brown, glossy, and carry many very visible lenticels. In old age, the branches take on a grayish tint and the bark cracks into numerous wrinkles. The black poplar and the Lombardy poplar prefer moist soil, deep and alkaline. In dry ground, they grow with much difficulty, and the Lombardy poplar especially withers in dry regions, becoming sensitive to disease. While the black poplar lives about three hundred years, the Lombardy poplar lives only for about fifty years. The terminal (twelve millimeters long) and auxiliary (six millimeters) buds, sticky and with curved tips, appear in the spring. The leaves, alternate, are deciduous, varying in form from oval to triangular shape, of light green, glabrous on both sides and glossy. In the autumn, they turn yellow.

HISTORY

The coloumnal Lombardy poplar, Populus nigra 'Italica' *or Poplar* fastigiata, *originated in northern Italy* before 1750, though it may have come from farther away, in Iran or Afghanistan; it was planted along canals in Europe to indicate structural works, like the succession of locks. The French writer and philosopher Jean-Jacques Rousseau planted it on an island on the Oise River in France, where he was buried in July 1778.

Use

Employed as an ornamental tree or as a signifier for artistic landscapes, the European and American black poplars of the *Aegeiros* section with all of their shapes and genetic improvements are often planted as fast-growing windbreaks or screens. In the past, the buds were used in an ointment to fight inflammation and chapped skin.

The Branch

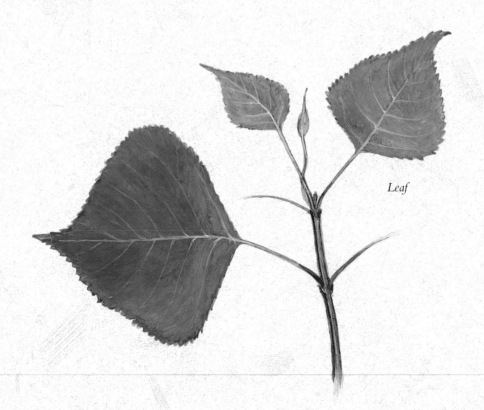

Leaf

YOUR LOMBARDY POPLAR LEAF

PLACE COLLECTED : _____

DATE COLLECTED : _____

COLLECTOR'S NAME : _____

NOTES : _____

_____

_____

GRAY POPLAR

- Populus x canescens (Ait.) Smith
- Salicaceae, willow family
- Place of origin: Natural hybrid, Europe
- Habitat: Country hedges, rows, parks

Etymology

It is interesting to note that the Latin word populus *means both "poplar" and "people."* Many hypotheses have been advanced as to the origin of this connection, including that this tree decorated public places, or that the foliage of the poplar is constantly in movement, like people always going this way and that. In Roman mythology, the white poplar (*Populus alba*) was traditionally consecrated to Hercules.

Interestingly, in many works on the art of gardens during the eighteenth century, the abele (now a name for the white poplar) is an elm (*Ulmus*) and not a poplar! All the species of the genus *Populus*, the poplar, are of the family Salicaceae, as is the willow (*Salix*).

Description

The gray poplar, Populus x canescens *(Ait.) Smith, is a natural hybrid between the white poplar or abele,* Populus alba L., and the European alder, *P. tremula* L., with many intermediary forms between the two parents. A fast grower, it can reach sixty-five to eighty feet in height. It is resistant to wind and to temporary drops in ground water. The young branches are gray. The deciduous leaves are alternate, with long petioles, and are borne on long branches. Two to four inches long, the oval to triangular leaves are dark green, grayish on the top, and have a gray to almost white downy or felted surface underneath.

A Few Other Species

The hairy-fruited poplar, Populus lasiocarpa Oliv., *which originated in China, is often planted in parks or allées.* Its leaves, remarkable for their size of almost a foot long and eight inches wide, are a very decorative dark green in color, glabrous on top and pale green underneath, and with the petiole and the principle red vein on the side exposed to the sun.

The balsam poplar or tacamahac, *Populus balsamifera* L. or *P. candicans* Ait., in the section *Tacamahacca* and native to northern North America, exudes from its buds a resin with a strong balsamic odor, known under the name of balm-of-Gilead or balm of Canada, used as a home remedy for coughs. Its offshoots are downy with jagged branches. The leaves, six inches long and four inches wide, are dark green on top, whitish and pubescent underneath.

POPLAR FLOWERS ARE FOR THE MOST PART INSIGNIFICANT. THEY APPEAR IN THE FORM OF CATKINS THAT GROW SEVERAL INCHES LONG AND EMERGE IN MARCH AND APRIL, LONG BEFORE THE ARRIVAL OF THE NEW LEAVES. THE FEMALE FLOWERS AND MALE FLOWERS APPEAR ON DIFFERENT TREES, SO THE POPLAR IN EFFECT IS DIOECIOUS. IN SPRING, THE FEMALE CATKINS ARE BLOWN AWAY, OFTEN COVERING THE GROUND BENEATH THE TREES IN A DOWNY, WHITISH CARPET.

THE BRANCH

Leaf

Your Gray Poplar Leaf

Place collected : _____

Date collected : _____

Collector's name : _____

Notes : _____

_____

_____

SWEET CHERRY

- PRUNUS AVIUM L.
- ROSACEAE, ROSE FAMILY
- OTHER COMMON NAMES: MAZZARD CHERRY, BIRD CHERRY
- PLACE OF ORIGIN: EUROPE
- HABITAT: HEDGES, WOODS, PARKS

GENERAL INFORMATION OF THE GENUS PRUNUS

The genus Prunus, *of the rose family, Rosaceae, is a "multiform" genus regrouping many stone fruit trees* that were previously classified in several genera according to their different uses in arboriculture: Prunus for plums, *Cerasus* for cherries, *Persica* for peaches, *Armeniaca* for apricots, *Amygdalus* for almonds, and *Laurocerasus* for cherry laurel. More than 200 species—some authors identify at least 430—and thousands of varieties and cultivars are listed from all the continents of the Northern Hemisphere, mostly in the temperate zones. Many species, often the large trees, appear spontaneously in the hot and humid tropical regions of Africa, Madagascar, Indonesia, New Guinea, and so on.

All *Prunus* species are either trees or shrubs, but a large majority are deciduous. Some, like the cherry laurel, *Prunus laurocerasus* L., or the Portugal laurel, *P. lusitanica* L., are evergreen. The genus includes a large number of ornamental trees, with a multitude of variations in outline, habit, period of flowering, and leaf color. In some countries, like Japan, festivals are organized around the blossoming of the cherry tree. Many stone fruit species have a common Chinese origin and were introduced during antiquity in Persia before spreading across the Mediterranean basin.

DESCRIPTION

The sweet cherry, Prunus avium *L., previously called* Cerasus avium *(L.) Moench, originates in Europe* and the Near East, where it grows in forests of conifers and leafy trees, often on the border of large forests. It can reach eighty feet in height. The branches have a brownish red bark at first, later becoming glossy and streaked. The leaves are deciduous, alternate, oval, crudely dentate at the edge, dark green, and four to six inches long. In autumn, they turn a pretty shade varying from yellow-orange to red. The white flowers appear before the new leaves in April in small bunches. The fruit, which matures in June and July, is blackish red like the common or wild cherry, and rather sour. A hardy tree, with a distinct preference for clay soil, it can live eighty to ninety years.

USES

The sweet cherry is sought after for cabinetmaking due to the quality of its wood. It was extensively used in the preceding centuries for the making of furniture, but the erosion of embankments and increasing rarity of hedges has caused a shortage. Many cultivars, some with double flowers, are used as ornamentals in parks and gardens. Some fruiting forms produce the small and dark *guigne* cherry (used to make the liqueur kirsch) and the larger white-heart cherry.

FORMING A SMALL TREE WITH A DENSE CROWN, ROUND AND REGULARLY BRANCHED, THE DOUBLE-FLOWERED FORM PRUNUS AVIUM "PLENA" BEARS SPECTACULAR SPRING BLOSSOM (END OF APRIL TO MAY). ITS DOUBLE SNOWY WHITE FLOWERS MEASURE THREE-QUARTERS TO ONE INCH AND ARE GROUPED IN DENSE CLUSTERS.

THE BRANCH

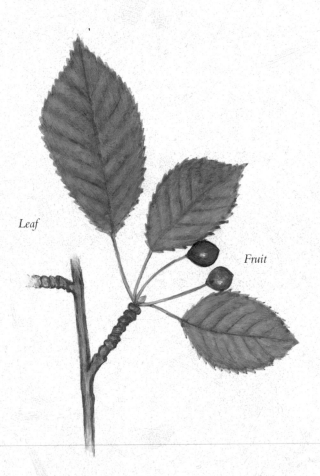

Leaf

Fruit

Your Sweet Cherry Leaf

Place collected : _____

Date collected : _____

Collector's name : _____

Notes : _____

_____

_____

ST. LUCIE CHERRY

- PRUNUS MAHALEB L.
- ROSACEAE, ROSE FAMILY
- OTHER COMMON NAMES: MAHALEB, PERFUMED CHERRY
- PLACE OF ORIGIN: MEDITERRANEAN
- HABITAT: FORESTS, HEDGES, PARKS

GENERAL INFORMATION ON THE GENUS *PRUNUS*

All of the species in the genus Prunus *have flowers of a similar composition, with five sepals, five petals,* many stamens, and one pistil that gives rise to a single fruit with one stone. The white, pink, or red flowers are grouped in clusters or in a corymb. A yellow-flowering specimen is very rare, existing in a few Chinese collections. Most species bloom in spring, from mid-January (as with the Japanese flowering apricot, *Prunus mume* Siebold) to mid-May. The stone of the fruit is surrounded by an edible pulp in the cherry, the peach, the apricot, and the plum, in contrast to the almond, where it is the seed in the stone that is eaten. Some *Prunus* foliage, like that of the cherry laurel, *Prunus laurocerasus* L., and stones are toxic after grinding.

DESCRIPTION

The St. Lucie cherry originates from the Mediterranean region and the Near East. The word mahaleb is the name given to it by the Arabs. The common name St. Lucie cherry comes from the village or the abbey of Sainte-Lucie, in the Vosges, where it grows in abundance. In the wild, this species grows at the warm and dry edges of sparse conifer and leafy forests. It thrives in medium deep to thin soils, stony, clayey, and calcium-rich, where it reaches a height of about thirty-five feet. Its deciduous leaves are alternate, round to cordate, one and one-half to two inches long, and green and smooth on both sides. They show no autumn color. The flowers, which appear before the leaves, are white, grouped in corymbs, and fragrant. The fruits vary from dark red to black in maturity and are edible but bitter. They are much appreciated by birds.

USES

The St. Lucie cherry's light red, pleasant-smelling, and long-lasting wood is much used in the making of pipes and canes. It is also often used as grafting stock for a variety of fruit trees.

OTHER SPECIES

The black or wild cherry, Prunus serotina *Ehrh., is the largest and most important native North American* cherry. Its wood is particularly valuable for professional and scientific instruments. Wild cherry syrup, a cough medicine, is obtained from its bark, and jelly and wine are prepared from its fruit. One of the first New World trees introduced into English gardens, it was recorded as early as 1629.

A CULINARY USE FOR THE ST. LUCIE CHERRY, SIMPLE BUT REFINED: A GREEN LEAF OR TWO DRIED LEAVES OF FRAGRANT CHERRY GIVE AN EXCELLENT AROMA TO A PARTRIDGE ROASTED ON A SPIT.

THE BRANCH

Leaf

Fruit

YOUR ST. LUCIE CHERRY LEAF

Place collected : _____

Date collected : _____

Collector's name : _____

Notes : _____
_____
_____

Scarlet Oak

- Quercus coccinea Muenchh.
- Fagaceae, beech family
- Place of origin: North America
- Habitat: Parks, urban street plantings, forest groves

General Information on the Genus Quercus

The genus Quercus, *the oak genus, contains many species, 250 to 300 or even 600, depending on the* authority, and many natural hybrids and cultivars. Though some of them originate from temperate zones of the Northern Hemisphere, others live in the tropical regions of South America and Southeast Asia. The large majority of oaks are trees, very often having a majestic crown, but there a few shrubs, like the California scrub oak (*Q. dumosa* Nutt.) or the chinquapin oak found from Maine to Alaska and Texas (*Q. prinoides* Willd.). Depending on the species, the foliage can be evergreen, deciduous, or semievergreen. The shape, dimension, texture, and color of the simple and alternate leaves vary.

Description

About eighty species originate from America, sixty of which are trees. These species are divided into four sections: *Phellos* (weeping oaks), *Albae* (white oaks), *Nigrae* (black oaks), and *Rubrae* (red oaks). It is in this last section, the red oaks, that one finds *Quercus coccinea* Meunchh., the scarlet oak. Its common name comes from the color of its foliage, particularly striking in autumn, partially marcescent up to Christmas. The deciduous leaves are alternate, four to eight inches long, and with six to eight coarsely dentate lobes. They are bright green on both sides before turning their autumnal color. The acorn has a short peduncle about three-quarters of an inch long, and is enclosed at its base by a cupule. The scarlet oak reaches eighty feet in height, with long and slender red-orange branches and large downy buds.

Many American oaks of the section *rubrae* are also often planted in parks or in rows, like the red oak, *Quercus rubra* L., or the pin oak, *Quercus palustris* Meunchh. The latter, though it prefers deep moist soil, can grow equally well in normal and even dry soil. Its leaves, of variable shape, are three to six inches long, with toothed lobes. In autumn, the glossy foliage is bedecked with a great range of colors, from scarlet-red to brown. The acorns, rather small, are wider than they are long.

Uses

The heavy, hard wood of the various oaks has been used for making a range of products, from baskets for the cotton fields and shingles for pioneer's houses to sturdy furniture and railroad cross ties. The timber from the live oak, *Quercus virginiana* Mill., was once important for building ships, and the nation's first publicly owned timber lands were purchased as early as 1799 for this purpose. The yellow oak, *Quercus velutina* Lam., was formerly a source of tannin (as was the chestnut oak, *Quercus prinus* L.), used in medicine and as a yellow dye for cloth. The white oak, *Quercus alba* L., is also called stave oak because its wood is outstanding for making tight barrels for whiskey and other liquids.

THE NATIVE AMERICANS OF THE FAR WESTERN UNITED STATES TRADITIONALLY TRANSFORMED THE BITTER ACORNS OF THE OAK TREE INTO AN EDIBLE, THOUGH RATHER TASTELESS, FLOUR. THE ACORNS WERE FIRST BOILED AND THEN STORED IN BASKETS. THE BASKETS WERE LEFT TO SOAK FOR MANY DAYS IN A RIVER. THIS LENGTHY SOAKING WASHED THE BITTERNESS AWAY AND THE ACORNS COULD THEN BE CRUSHED INTO FLOUR.

THE BRANCH

Leaf

Fruit

Your Scarlet Oak Leaf

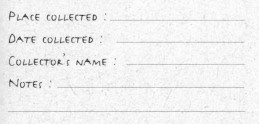

Place collected : _____

Date collected : _____

Collector's name : _____

Notes : _____

_____

_____

Holm Oak

- Quercus ilex L.
- Fagaceae, beech family
- Other common names: Holly oak
- Place of origin: Mediterranean
- Habitat: Mediterranean forests, parks, gardens

Etymology

Though the Romans originally called this oak quercus, *from which comes its Latin genus name, its common* name of holly oak comes from its species name, *ilex*. In the eighteenth century, the Swedish botanist Linnaeus assigned the genus name of *Ilex* to the holly, but he called the holm oak, or holly oak, *Quercus ilex*. It is not always easy to understand botanical logic. The English word *oak* comes from the Old English *ac* and is perhaps related to the Greek *aigilops*, a kind of oak.

Origin

Most of the evergreen oaks originate in the tropical and subtropical regions around the Mediterranean. Among the species of this region, one finds the kermes oak (*Quercus coccifera* L.), a shrub that does not reach more than ten feet in height and grows in scrublands. The cork oak (*Quercus suber* L.) is a tree of great stature, at least in optimal conditions, given warmth, ample sunlight, and some rainfall. The most widespread oak in Europe, especially in the Atlantic zone, is unquestionably the holm oak, *Quercus ilex*. One of the most impressive and most remarkable specimens has lived for centuries in the garden of the University of Saint Andrews, in Scotland.

Description

The holm oak rarely grows more than fifty feet tall. It is known to grow very slowly (ten feet every twenty years), but it can live for more than a thousand years! With its short trunk, it creates thick and dense forests, covering the forest floor in dead leaves.

The holm oak's foliage is evergreen, with each leaf remaining two to three years on the tree before falling. Dark green in color, the leaves are glabrous and glossy on top, and gray and downy underneath. They are variable in form, elliptical to orbicular, one to two inches long, dentate, with a short petiole, toothed when young, and entire when mature. The flowers appear in April and May; the male catkins are drooping, while the female flowers appear in clusters. The acorn is long and embraced by a cupule of triangular shells, which enclose about half of the nut.

Uses

The heavy, durable, close-grained wood of the holm oak polishes well, and is therefore used in cabinetmaking. Some species of oak possess soft, edible acorns, which are boiled before being ground into flour. Though it has usually been restricted to periods of famine, this use of the acorn can be seen in some rural regions of the Middle East, with *Q. macrolepis* Kotschy, and among the Native Americans of California with the valley oak, *Q. lobata* Née. The thickened bark, or cork, of the cork oak, *Q. suber* L., has been used throughout the Mediterranean basin since antiquity for wine stoppers and a multitude of other uses.

It is not always easy to distinguish a young Holm oak tree from the common holly shrub (*Ilex aquifolium*) because their foliage is so very similar. Both the Holm oak and the holly bear evergreen, alternate leaves that are irregular and undulating, and more or less toothed.

THE BRANCH

Fruit

Leaf

Your Holm Oak Leaf

Place collected : _____

Date collected : _____

Collector's name : _____

Notes : _____

_____

_____

English Oak

- Quercus robur L.
- Fagaceae, beech family
- Other common names: Truffle oak
- Place of origin: Northern Europe
- Habitat: Forests, parks

HISTORY

Due to its longevity—individual specimens can live many centuries—the oak has been honored by many civilizations, including the Gauls, Irish, Greeks, and Germans. According to Virgil, the oak is the emblem of the god of the laws governing heaven and hell; the Germans attributed the oak to Donar, the god of tempests. With the Greeks, the oak leaf honors winners of the Olympic Games. In Rome, the same leaf rewards civic virtues, and the tradition has been perpetuated in the form of an ornament on the kepi, a military cap used in France. The Celts held that the oak, along with the apple tree, was one of the most important trees, at once the mother of all trees and the tree of the supreme deity.

ORIGIN

The English oak, Quercus robur *L. or Q.* pendunculata *Ehrh., which originated in Northern Europe* and the Middle East, grows in deep, well-drained clay soils. Dozens of other oak species grow in North America. The Arkansas oak, *Quercus arkansana* Sarg., an uncommon oak, is thought to be an ancient species of formerly wider distribution in the Coastal Plain. The southern red oak, *Quercus falcata* Michx., is also called Spanish oak because it commonly occurs in areas of the early Spanish colonies, though it is unlike any oaks native to Spain. The bur oak, *Quercus macrocarpa* Michx., is the northernmost New World oak and sports the largest acorns of all native oaks.

DESCRIPTION

The English oak can reach sixty-five to eighty feet in height, with a similar span across. Its leaves have rounded lobes, four to six inches long and two to three inches wide, and are a deep green color that is lighter on the backside. Ranging from yellow to brown in autumn, they are marcescent, remaining on the tree for most of the winter. The peduncle of the leaf is short, though that of the acorn is very long (two to five inches) in contrast to the Durmast oak, *Q. petraea* (Matt.) Liebl., where the leaf has a peduncle but the acorn has none at all.

USES

The English oak supplied timbers for the ships of the Royal Navy and oak paneling for famous buildings.

The bark was formerly a source of tannin.

AMONG THE VARIETY OF NATURAL FORMS OF THE ENGLISH OAK, Q. ROBUR L. 'FASTIGIATA' HAS BEEN SELECTED BY NURSERYMEN FOR ITS REMARKABLE COLUMNAR HABIT. WITH ITS ERECT AND THICK BRANCHES, IT CAN REACH FIFTY TO SIXTY-FIVE FEET IN HEIGHT, WHILE REMAINING ONLY TEN OR TWELVE FEET ACROSS.

THE BRANCH

Fruit

Leaf

YOUR ENGLISH OAK LEAF

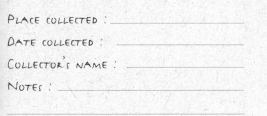

WHITE WILLOW

- Salix alba L.
- Salicaceae, willow family
- Place of origin: Europe, Asia
- Habitat: Parks, beside ponds and rivers

ETYMOLOGY

The scientific name Salix, the genus defined by botanist Joseph Pitton de Tournefort (1656–1708) at the end of the seventeenth century, comes from the Latin name for willow. Another name for the willow, osier, though very close to the Greek *oison*, which means willow, is Frankish in origin.

ORIGIN

The genus Salix, willow or osier, is made up of about three hundred species that essentially originate from the temperate and cold regions of the Northern Hemisphere. Though some species are found in the Southern Hemisphere, none grow in Australia. The diversity of forms and habits of the willow (prostrate, creeping, erect, weeping, and so on) is immense. The height of the woody plants varies from a few inches for the species of the polar regions and high mountains to a hundred feet or more for those in humid forests.

In spite of this diversity, all of the species are deciduous with alternate, entire leaves with short petioles, in shapes varying from elliptical to linear or lanceolate. The leaves appear very early in spring, often before those of other species. The male and female flowers, held differently on their stalks, appear in spring in sessile catkins, before the new leaves in some species, like the pussy willow, *Salix caprea* L., or at the same time, as in the white willow.

DESCRIPTION

The white willow, Salix alba, is a large tree, growing as tall as seventy-five feet in height. Originating from a vast region from Europe to Asia, it is characteristically found by ponds and rivers or among alders (*Alnus* sp.), poplars (*Populus* sp.), and other species of willows in humid forests. It is a fast grower, with somewhat flexible erect, brown-yellow or reddish branches. The mature trunks are gray, with deeply wrinkled bark. The lanceolate leaves can measure up to four inches long. The flowers have a very characteristic bluish gray color, due to the play between the gray and dark gray-green on the top of the leaves and the blue underneath; both sides are covered in silvery and silky down.

USES

Introduced from Europe to North America in colonial times, the white willow was planted as a shade and ornamental tree and for shelterbelts, fenceposts, and fuel. Its colorful twigs have been used to make baskets, and one variety in England is prized for cricket bats. The bark of the two- to three-year-old branches of the white willow contain salicin, used for medicinal salicylic acid. Another widely known species of willow, the weeping willow, *Salix babylonica* L., with its supple weeping branches, originated in central Asia and was introduced in Europe to the west during the seventeenth century.

THE BRANCH

Leaf

YOUR WHITE WILLOW LEAF

PLACE COLLECTED : _____

DATE COLLECTED : _____

COLLECTOR'S NAME : _____

NOTES : _____

_____

_____

Mountain Ash

- Sorbus torminalis (L.) Crantz
- Rosaceae, rose family
- Other common names: Wild service tree, rowan tree
- Place of origin: Asia Minor, North Africa
- Habitat: Parks, gardens, urban rows

ETYMOLOGY

The word ash *comes from the Old English word* asce *and is related to the Sanskrit* asa, *mreaning dry. Our* word *arid* is of the same origin. Another name for the mountain ash is the *rowan* tree; the word rowan is derived from an old Scandinavian word meaning "red," referring to the tree's brightly colored berries. Roan Mountain, North Carolina/Tennessee, may have been named for the mountain ash or rowan trees along its summit.

ORIGIN

The genus Sorbus *is made up of eighty to one hundred species, depending on the author, all of which* originate from the Northern Hemisphere and can be considered to be wild fruit trees or shrubs. This complex genus is subdivided into several different sections, according to leaves. Thus, one section, the *Aria*, includes species with simple leaves originating from cold and mountain zones, and the *Sorbus* section represents species with composite leaves with an odd number of leaflets, originating from the plains. The wild service tree, *Sorbus torminalis* (L.) Crantz, is an example from the *Aria* section; the service tree, *Sorbus domestica* L. (see page 154), belongs to the *Sorbus* section. Originally from southern Europe, Asia Minor, and North Africa, *Sorbus torminalis*, the mountain ash or wild service tree grows on dry, warm, sunny slopes among deciduous forests of durmast oaks, *Quercus petraea* L. Though it is indifferent to soil pH, whether chalky or lightly acidic, the ash does not like sandy or moist soil. It prefers regions with mild winters.

DESCRIPTION

Growing rapidly when young but slowing as it matures, the mountain ash reaches about thirty-five feet with a rounded, spreading top, and can live two to three hundred years. The quarter-inch-long buds are a glabrous green bordering on brown. The deciduous leaves, alternate and simple, are as wide as they are long, divided into six to eight lobes, light green and more or less satiny and glabrous above, and gray-green underneath. In autumn, the leaves turn yellow-orange to red and on to brown-gold. The flowers are white in erect panicles, three to nearly five inches in length, and appear in May and June. The fruit, ovoid, brown, and covered in large lenticels, is edible but bitter.

OTHER SPECIES

The American mountain ash, Sorbus americana *Marsh., is native to the moist valleys and slopes of the* Appalachian Mountains from north Georgia up to Newfoundland, and west to northern Illinois. It has smooth gray bark and pinnately compound leaves, which turn yellow in the fall. A handsome ornamental, its showy red fruit persists into winter and is much appreciated by birds.

USES

The wood of the mountain ash, reddish white, is durable, heavy, and very even-textured. Easy to work with and polish, it is used by woodturners and in the making of tools. It is also the best wood with which to make baseball bats. The Romans used this tree's fruit as a remedy against colic and dysentery.

THE BRANCH

Fruit

Leaf

Your Mountain Ash Leaf

Place collected : _____

Date collected : _____

Collector's name : _____

Notes : _____

_____

_____

LINDEN

- Tilia cordata Mill.
- Tiliaceae, linden family
- Other common names: European littleleaf - linden, basswood, lime tree, whitewood
- Place of origin: Europe
- Habitat: Forests, parks, rows

ETYMOLOGY AND HISTORY

The word tilia *has a rather obscure origin; some believe that is from the Greek* tilai, *"small bits of wool or* fibers," since in earlier days its bark was used for its fibers. The word *linden* is probably related to the Old English word *lithe*, meaning "gentle," and can be traced back to the Latin *lentus*, meaning "slow." One often finds this tree in legends and traditional songs of Germany and Central Europe, and in the city and village squares of Europe justice was meted out under the foliage of the linden, which could be hundreds of years old, if not a thousand.

ORIGIN

The genus Tilia *is made up of more than thirty species with natural habitats in Europe, Near East,* Far East, the forests of southeastern North America, and Mexico. In nature, different *Tilia* species hybridize quite easily.

DESCRIPTION

Growing from the plains to up to 5,000 feet above sea level, the European littleleaf linden, Tilia cordata, can reach more than eighty feet, with a spread of fifty to sixty-five feet. Its glabrous and glossy branches are brownish red at first before they become a bronzed brown. The leaves, alternate and deciduous, are round or cordiate, and often broader than long (one to four inches), with a petiole of one to two inches. They are dark green above and bluish gray-green underneath, with reddish auxiliary tufts along the principal and secondary veins. In autumn, the leaves turn a beautiful luminous gold. Unlike the majority of the trees in the temperate regions of Europe, the linden flowers in summer, at the beginning of July. Its yellowish white flowers appear in groups of five to seven on cymes, at the end of a peduncle connected to a wing-shaped bract one and one-half to a little over three inches long. The fruits, which resemble small oval or round nuts with a brown down or felt, ripen in October.

USES

The linden is valuable as a good source of nectar for honeybees, and linden honey is much prized.
Since antiquity, linden flowers have been collected and dried to be used in teas for their calming and refreshing qualities. The linden is also a valuable shade tree and ornamental, but many species are infected in the summer, especially in urban conditions, by aphids that cover the leaves in sticky honeydew.

THE WOOD OF THE AMERICAN LINDEN (TILIA AMERICANA L.), OTHERWISE KNOWN AS THE AMERICAN BASSWOOD, IS SOFT AND LIGHT AND ESPECIALLY USEFUL FOR MAKING YARDSTICKS, FURNITURE, AND ANY WORDWORKING THAT REQUIRES CARVING. IT IS SOMETIMES ALSO CALLED THE BEE TREE, AS IT IS FAVORED BY BEES AND PRODUCES A STRONGLY FLAVORED HONEY.

THE BRANCH

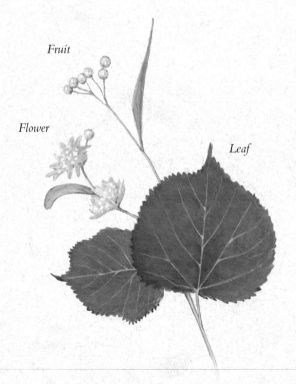

Fruit

Flower

Leaf

YOUR LINDEN LEAF

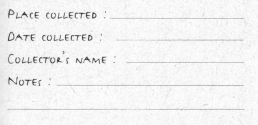

English Elm

- Ulmus procera Salisb.
- Ulmaceae, elm family
- Place of origin: Europe
- Habitat: Village hedges, parks

Etymology

The Latin genus name Ulmus *was that used by the Romans for this tree and is the origin of our word* elm.
The French word *orme* comes from a Celtic word for cutting, as according to the Latin author
Strabon, the Gauls used the wood of the elm to make javelins.

Origins and History

The twenty species and their natural hybrids of the genus Ulmus *originate from the temperate regions of*
the Northern Hemisphere. All are deciduous semievergreen trees with simple, alternate, and
asymmetrical leaves.

In France, at the end of the sixteenth century, the king decreed the planting of elms along
the grand streets and malls of urban areas. It is often under this species that justice was meted out.
The first large plantings in the park of Versailles, during the seventeenth century, were composed
of elms, and made up the grand palisades, which replaced the hornbeams (*Carpinus*) used earlier.
The American elm, *Ulmus americana* L., was once familiar on lawns and city streets throughout
North America, before being ravaged by the Dutch elm disease, accidentally introduced in 1930.

Description

Ulmus procera Salisb.*, also known as* U. campestris L.*, is known under the common name English elm.*
Originating from the southern and eastern parts of Europe, as well as North Africa and Asia
Minor, the elm can surpass one hundred feet in height, with a slender and straight trunk. The
smooth, reedy branches are brown or reddish brown with pointed, dark brown conical buds.
Twisted and undulating, the branches spread out like a fan. In old age, ligneous outgrowths can
appear on the deeply furrowed gray bark. The leaves, oval, simple, very asymmetrical, three to four
inches long by one and one-half to two inches wide, and double dentate, are dark green on top
and pale and pubescent in the vein angles underneath. The insignificant red flowers appear before
the leaves in February and March. The fruit ripens a few weeks after the blossoms and is a one-
seeded samara with a greenish-yellow wing surrounding the nutlet and usually notched at the
apex. In autumn, the leaves turn a bright yellow.

Uses

The thick, fragrant, edible, gluelike inner bark of the red elm, Ulmus rubra *Muhl., was traditionally dried* and afterward moistened for use as a cough medicine or as a poultice. The wood of the rock elm, *Ulmus thomasii* Sarg., is hard and tough, which makes it particularly useful for agricultural tools and handles. In the nineteenth century, the durable timber was exported to England for battleships and sailing vessels. In North America in the eighteenth and nineteenth centuries, the fibrous inner bark of the winged elm, *Ulmus alata* Michx., or *wahoo* as the Creek Indians called it, was made into rope for fastening covers of cotton bales.

> To differentiate between the leaves of the elm and the hornbeam (*Carpinus*), just tear the leaf along the central vein. The two sides of the elm leaf will not overlap very well, while those of the hornbeam will match perfectly.

The Branch

Leaf

Your English Elm Leaf

PLACE COLLECTED : _____

DATE COLLECTED : _____

COLLECTOR'S NAME : _____

NOTES : _____
_____
_____

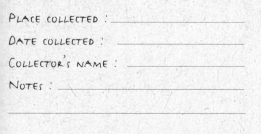

Compound Leaves

The compound leaf is one that is composed of two or more small independent leaves known as leaflets. Each leaflet can be detached from the principle axis, without damaging the other leaflets. These leaflets can be alternately or oppositely placed along the axis, in pairs or singly.

Opposite

Leaves are called opposite when they are paired two on a node at opposite sides of an axis or stem.

Alternate

Leaves are called alternate when they are arranged singly at different heights and on different sides of the axis or stem.

Box Elder

- Acer negundo L.
- Aceraceae, maple family
- Other common names: Ashleaved maple
- Place of origin: North America
- Habitat: Parks, gardens

GENERAL INFORMATION ON THE GENUS ACER

It is not always easy to find one's way through all the shapes and colors of maples offered by nurseries. Depending on the species, the height varies from fifteen feet to over sixty-five, so it is necessary first to choose a species that will work in the space that you plan for it. Secondly, there are a variety of colors and textures to the barks, like the striped maple, *A. pensylvanicum* L., which has green trunks conspicuously striped with white. Some species or their cultivars have foliage of diverse colors—variegated white, gold, purple, and purple that turns green in the summer—or deeply serrated, like some Japanese species, like *A. palmatum* Thunb. and its cultivars. In the autumn, the colors turn from red to orange and on to gold. The genus *Acer* is one of the few that can offer so much ornamental diversity.

ORIGIN

Originating from the sides of lakes and moist prairies, Acer negundo L., *the box elder or ashleaved maple,* covers a large part of the continent of North America, and some authors distinguish many subspecies. It was introduced to Europe, where it not only acclimated but also naturalized, at the end of the seventeenth century, with many other species from the East Coast of the United States and Canada.

DESCRIPTION

A tree of medium width and reaching fifty to sixty-five feet in height, the box elder's branches are bright green, sometimes covered with a waxy, bluish coating, or "bloom." The deciduous leaves are opposite, and composed of three to five leaflets that are bright green on top. The terminal leaflets are sometimes themselves made of many lobes. The flowers, pale green, appear in March and April before the tree leafs out in pendulous corymbs, very compact for the male flowers. The samaras, or winged fruit, have greenish white wings and are grouped in clusters.

OTHER SPECIES

Many cultivars of Acer negundo are planted, such as 'Aureo-Variegatum', *with dark green leaflets variegated* with irregular golden yellow spots, 'Variegatum', with white edges, and 'Flamingo', with leaflets punctuated by light pink spots. Other maples with composite leaves are rare and found mainly in specialty gardens and arboretums.

THE COMMON NAME "BOX ELDER" INDICATES THE RESEMBLANCE OF THIS TREE'S FOLIAGE TO THAT OF THE ELDER (SAMBUCUS), AND THE SIMILARITY OF ITS WHITISH WOOD TO THAT OF THE BOX, BUXUS SEMPERVIRENS L.

THE BRANCH

Leaf

Fruit

Your Box Elder Leaf

Place collected : _____
Date collected : _____
Collector's name : _____
Notes : _____
_____
_____

European Ash

- *Fraxinus excelsior L.*
- *Oleaceae*, olive family
- Place of origin: Europe
- Habitat: Rural hedges, parks

Etymology and History

Fraxinus *is the word used by the Romans for the ash tree. The ash appears in Greek mythology, devoted to* the cult of Poseidon, as well as in Germanic and Scandinavian mythologies. It is a cosmic tree: its top reaches the celestial heavens, its roots plunge down into the underworld. The Celts also honored it. A druid's rod dating from the first century B.C., found in Anglesey, Great Britain, is made of ash. In Ireland, its wood has the power to protect against drowning, and many Irish emigrants to the United States carried branches of the sacred ash of Killura. Up until the nineteenth century, infants affected by hernias were carried naked to the top of an ash tree before sunrise to cure them.

Origin

This genus, Fraxinus, *which shares the family Oleaceae with the olive (Olea), is made up of more than* sixty-five species spread out over all the regions of the temperate and subtropical Northern Hemisphere. It is made up in general of large trees, except for a few shrubby species. Depending on the species, deep and cool or very dry soil is necessary for the ash to thrive. Preferring full sun, it can nevertheless be grown in partial shade. One single American species is evergreen. The leaves are opposite and composite, with a varying number of odd leaflets. In winter, large bulging buds appear, their color varying depending on the species from black to gray or brown. The fruit is a one-seeded, winged samara.

Description

The European ash, Fraxinus excelsior L., *is the most widespread species of the genus, ranging from* Europe in the west to the Caucasus and Iran. In the Alps, it is found up to 5,000 feet above sea level. A large tree can reach more than a hundred feet in height, with a spread of sixty-five to one hundred feet; its leaves sometimes measure nearly six inches long, with nine to thirteen opposite leaflets two to five inches in length and three-quarters of an inch to two inches across. The fruit, ripe in September, is grouped in clusters that often remain on the tree until spring. The flowering ash or manna ash, *Faxinus ornus* L., which originates in the south of Europe and the Near East, is small in size, with leaves six to eight inches long made of seven leaflets. It is adorned with very beautiful and fragrant blossoms in large, six-inch-long terminal panicles in May and June. Its fruit resembles small winged nuts.

USES

At once practical and symbolic, the coracles, traditional Irish boats of the past, had oars and laths of ash.
Today, because of the strength of its wood, the European ash is often used for furniture, decorations, sporting goods, and tool handles. In prolonged drought, when grass becomes scarce, ash leaves are used as forage for livestock. In the warm regions of Italy the manna ash exudes a sweet greenish substance called manna, which is used as a purgative.

THE BRANCH

Fruit   Leaf

YOUR EUROPEAN ASH LEAF

Place collected : _____

Date collected : _____

Collector's name : _____

Notes : _____
_____
_____

Mimosa

- Albizia julibrissin (Durazz.) Willd.
- Leguminosae, pea family
- Other common names: Silk tree, powderpuff tree
- Place of origin: Iran
- Habitat: Parks, gardens

ETYMOLOGY

The first tree of the genus Albizia *(sometimes spelled* Albizzia*) was introduced in 1745 in Constantinople,* from where derives its ancient name acacia of Constantinople. The botanist Antonio Durazzini, who first described the new tree, named it after the man who introduced it, the naturalist and Italian botanist the Knight of Albizzi, from a powerful family of Florence. It is interesting to note that *julibrissin*, the species name of the most ancient *Albizia* species in western Europe, is the Persian word for "tree." The common name mimosa was given to this tree because it resembles the herbaceous sensitive plant, *Mimosa pudica* L., whose leaves fold up when touched; the mimosa tree's leaves fold up at night.

HABITAT

The genus Albizia *is made up of about 100 to 125 species that originate from the tropical and subtropical* regions of Asia, Africa, and Australia, with one species from Mexico. The great majority of these plants were brought to Europe and America during the nineteenth century; most of them are not hardy, with the exception of the mimosa, *Albizia julibrissin*, and the woman's-tongue tree, *A. lebbeck* (L.) Benth., which is cultivated only around the Côte d'Azur. The most widely known species in our climate is *A. julibrissin*. Though it grows without difficulty in Mediterranean climates and in the southeastern United States, it needs a protected and sunny spot in other regions. Remember, it originally came from Iran.

DESCRIPTION

This is a small tree, only reaching forty feet or so in height, though its branches spread out with age, giving it an umbrella-like habit that can make it a useful shade tree. The alternate leaves are large; six to twelve pairs of fine secondary ramifications each carry twenty to thirty pairs of small, light green leaflets. The leaves resemble those of a fern. It blooms in summer between June and September, with pale pink or white flowers in big silky pompoms with long and brilliant stamens. The fruits are drooping pods about two inches long.

Uses

With its habit and exotic flowers, the silk tree is often used as a small ornamental specimen. It requires good garden soil and a warm and sheltered position in order to flower well.

THE TRAITÉ DE L'ORANGERIE DES SERRES CHAUDES ET CHÂSSIS (TREATISE ON THE ORANGERIE OF GREENHOUSES AND COLD FRAMES, 1788) HAS THE FOLLOWING COMMENTARY ON THE MIMOSA, OR ACACIA OF CONSTANTINOPLE: "SINCE WE POSSESS ONLY YOUNG INDIVIDUALS OF THIS ACACIA, WE CAN NOT EVEN SAY IF IT IS A SMALL TREE, OR A LARGE TREE; AND IF AN ORANGERIE IS NECESSARY FOR IT, OR IF IT CAN GROW IN THE OPEN SOIL, WHERE IT MIGHT GROW LARGE. ONE CAN OBSERVE ONLY THAT IT LIKES EXPOSURE TO MORNING SUN."

THE BRANCH

Leaf

Flower

YOUR MIMOSA LEAF

Place collected : _____

Date collected : _____

Collector's name : _____

Notes : _____

_____

_____

English Walnut

- Juglans regia L.
- Juglandaceae, walnut family
- Place of origin: Middle East, Central Asia
- Habitat: Plantations, parks

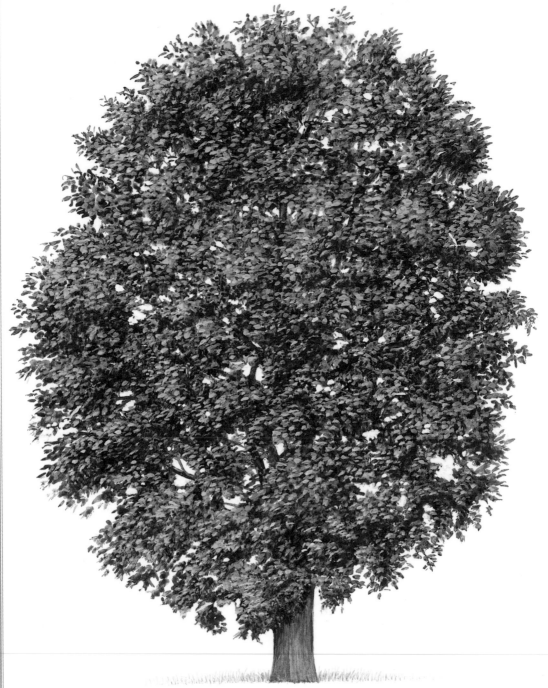

ETYMOLOGY

The genus names Juglans *derives from* Jovis glans, *"acorn or fruit of God, divine fruit," because of its taste,* especially when compared to the oak (*Quercus*). In contrast, the Greeks called it *karna*, derived from *kana*, "head," because they believed that the nut "gives off a vapor that slows the head down and is mind-numbing." The English common name *walnut* is Germanic in origin and means "foreign nut."

ORIGIN

Of the genus Juglans, *about fifteen deciduous species grow in the Northern Hemisphere, some from* southwestern Europe to Asia, others from North and South America. Mostly trees but sometimes shrubby, they have deciduous, alternate, and composite leaves, always with an odd number of leaflets. The flowers have separate sexes; the males form long catkins in April and May from the previous year's wood, while the female flowers appear on new wood. The fruit, which matures in autumn, is made up of a fleshy membrane, the husk, and a woody shell that contains the walnut halves. The main American species—the butternut or white walnut, *Juglans cinerea* L., and the black walnut, *J. nigra* L.—were introduced to England by John Tradescant in the year 1630. The black walnut is faster growing and less sensitive to spring frosts than the English walnut, as well as more ornamental and excellent for woodworking.

DESCRIPTION

The English walnut originates from the Caucasus, Persia, and from Central Asia to the western part of China. Cultivated since antiquity, it is naturalized in southern Europe and has been much planted as a nut tree in the warmer parts of the United States, particularly California. Able to reach eighty to a hundred feet in height, its boughs are substantial and round; its large branches end in spherical terminal buds that are greenish brown to black and covered with fine shells. The leaves create large cicatrices, and are of different shapes, depending on the cultivar. Eight to twelve inches long, they are made of five to nine leaflets each measuring two to five inches in length, either entire or dentate. The leaves are aromatic when crushed.

Uses

Though hardy, the English walnut is sensitive to spring frosts, though the American black walnut is less so.

Many cultivars have been selected for the qualities of their nuts, which have an oil content between 40 and 50 percent. The bark contains tannins, and the outer husks of the nuts are used to make a very long-lasting brown dye. Walnut wood, which is hard and polishes well, is among the most appreciated by cabinetmakers and carpenters, used especially for furniture, gunstocks, and veneer.

If the husks are collected while the nut is green and incompletely formed, a liqueur with digestive properties can be extracted from them. On the other hand, the husks of ripe nuts yield a long-lasting brown dye used by woodworkers.

The Branch

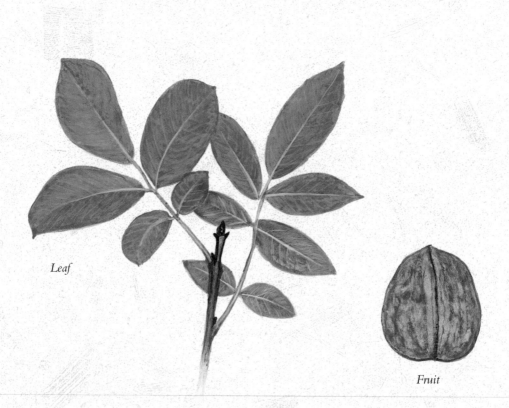

Leaf

Fruit

YOUR ENGLISH WALNUT LEAF

Place collected : _____

Date collected : _____

Collector's name : _____

Notes : _____

_____

_____

Caucasian Wingnut

- Pterocarya fraxinifolia (Lam.) Spach.
- Juglandaceae, walnut family
- Place of origin: Caucasus, Armenia
- Habitat: Parks, allées

Etymology

The genus name Pterocarya *is composed of two Greek words,* pteron, *"wing," and* carya, *"nut,"* characterizing the fruit surrounded by a large semicircular wing.

Origin

The eight known species, which belong to the walnut family, Juglandaceae, are all originally from Asia—six from China, one from Japan, and another from the humid forests of the region making up the Caucasus and Armenia. This last species was first introduced to France at the end of the eighteenth century by French botanist André Michaux after his long stay in the Middle East. The first specimens were planted in the gardens of Trianon, at Versailles. In North America, the Caucasian wingnut is an uncommon tree, most often found in large botanical parks; the Brooklyn Botanic Garden has a fine specimen.

Description

The Caucasian wingnut is a large tree that reaches more than sixty-five feet in height. In England, some specimens grow well over a hundred feet. The tree sprouts easily from its stump, and some old specimens have a larger diameter at ground level than at the top. The deciduous, alternate leaves are composite. They can measure up to six inches long, with an odd number of sessile leaflets, varying from thirteen to twenty-one, oval in shape or elongated to over three inches, and glossy dark green. The central vein is hairy. In autumn, the leaves turn yellow. The bark of the Caucasian wingnut becomes gray-black with age, developing long longitudinal cracks. The branches are olive brown to greenish gray in color. The male inflorescences reach more than eight inches in length. The fruits, small nuts three-eighths to three-quarters of an inch in diameter, with a semicircular wing, are arranged on long, slender, drooping spindles that can reach a length of nearly six inches.

USE

In deep, rich, moist soil conditions, with lots of sun, the Caucasian wingnut will grow quickly. It adapts to the very dry soil and polluted air found in cities, however, and has been planted as a street tree. It has a significant drawback, however; in moist soil, compact or impermeable, the shallow roots can stretch far out from under the crown.

THOUGH THE CAUCASIAN WINGNUT IS HARDY, ITS NEW LEAVES APPEAR EARLY AND CAN BE THREATENED BY EARLY FROSTS. ON THE OTHER HAND, IT IS GOOD AT COPING WITH URBAN POLLUTION, WIND, AND PROLONGED FLOODING.

THE BRANCH

Leaf

Your Caucasian Wingnut Leaf

Chinese Scholar Tree

- Sophora japonica L.
- Leguminosae, pea family
- Other common names: Japanese pagoda tree
- Place of origin: North China, Korea
- Habitat: Parks, urban street plantings

Etymology

The genus name Sophora *comes from the Arab word* sophera *or* sephira, *which designates another* tree in the same family, *Senna sophera*. The common name Japanese pagoda tree reflects the fact that in its native Orient, it is often grown around temples.

Origins

The genus Sophora *is made up of about sixty species originating from all the continents—as well as* New Zealand (*Sophora microphylla* Ait.) and Easter Island (*Sophora toromiro* Skottsb.)—though a very large majority come from the subtropical or tropical climates. Many species are hardy only in the South in the United States. Species may have deciduous or evergreen leaves, but they are always alternate and composite, with an odd number of leaflets.

The Chinese scholar tree, *Sophora japonica* L., also known as the Japanese pagoda tree, is originally from China and Korea. Since the first seeds were collected by Incarville, a French Jesuit living at the court of the emperor of China, and planted in France in 1747, it has been a coveted ornamental in parks and lining streets throughout the warmer areas of Europe and North America.

Description

The Chinese scholar tree is a large tree with raised principal branches and horizontal to drooping secondary branches; its young branches are covered in dark green bark, marked with many light brown lenticels. In spite of its short trunk, the tree can reach a height of sixty-five feet, with a large vaulted and airy rounded top and a spread of about fifty to sixty-five feet. The leaves, which measure up to ten inches long, have seven to seventeen oval, pointed leaflets, about two inches long. Green, more or less glossy on top and matte underneath with a slight pubescence, the leaves can turn a light yellow in the autumn. The tree leafs out late, sometimes as late as the beginning of June, and the leaves, still green, fall at the end of the first frost in autumn.

If the season is warm enough, the flowering, from the end of July to the beginning of August, can be spectacular. The trailingflower clusters, composed of golden flowers, measure eight inches to a foot long. The fruit, which ripens in October, is a long, hanging, yellowish pod two or three inches long, which narrows between each rounded triangular seed, giving the effect of a string of pearls.

USES

In northern China, a religious and imperial tree, the scholar tree can be found in many gardens and parks of monasteries, and can reach many hundreds of years old, even a thousand. The Chinese extract a yellow dye from the flower buds; the bark and other parts reportedly have medicinal properties. In America, it is used as a street tree for its ornamental quality and its soft shade. There is a small weeping cultivar, *S. japonica* 'Pendula', whose branches form a succession of superimposed arches, giving it a very picturesque shape in winter, especially when it is pruned regularly. Because of its shape, the Chinese call this form "witches claw."

THOUGH INTRODUCED TO EUROPE IN 1747, THE CHINESE SCHOLAR TREE REMAINED AN ENIGMA, AND BOTANISTS WERE UNCERTAIN FOR A LONG TIME WHAT TO NAME IT. NOT UNTIL THE FIRST BLOSSOMING, IN 1779, OF A SPECIMEN PLANTED IN THE GARDENS OF TRIANON AT VERSAILLES WAS THE PERMANENT NAME SOPHORA JAPONICA GIVEN TO THIS TREE.

THE BRANCH

Leaf

YOUR CHINESE SCHOLAR TREE LEAF

PLACE COLLECTED : _____

DATE COLLECTED : _____

COLLECTOR'S NAME : _____

NOTES : _____

_____

SERVICE TREE

- Sorbus domestica L.
- Rosaceae, rose family
- Other common names: Mountain ash, rowan tree
- Place of origin: Europe
- Habitat: Forests, gardens, urban street plantings

Etymology

The genus Sorbus *is divided into two large principal sections according to the species' foliage, one for* composite evergreens such as the service tree, *Sorbus domestica* L., and the other for entire evergreens like the wild service tree *Sorbus torminalis* (L.) Crantz. (page 116). The genus name *Sorbus* is the Latin name for the tree, specifically for *Sorbus domestica*. This word is probably Celtic in origin, and means "sour apple," which deftly describes the fruit of the service tree. The word *rowan*, derived from the old Scandinavian word meaning "red," refers to the tree's brightly colored berries.

Description

The service tree, Sorbus domestica, *sometimes* Cormus domestica *or* Pyrus domestica, *originated in the* south from Europe in the west to Asia in the east, and along North Africa. Cultivated since antiquity, the service tree is a slow grower, reaching sixty feet in a forest, taller when it is planted in an open space alone. It is a long-lived tree; it is possible to find specimens many centuries old. The branches are an olive green to brownish red color with glabrous buds, oval in shape. The deciduous, alternate leaves, about eight inches long, are made of thirteen to sixteen leaflets of one to three inches; the lowest three are smooth-edged, the upper ones dentate. Green on top, they are very light underneath and hairy along the veins. In autumn, their color varies from gold to orange. The white flowers, which appear in May and June, are grouped in corymbs. The fruits are one or two inches long, and look like small apples or pear; at first a yellow-green, they take on a pink tint when ripe. Edible but very sour, these fruits are sometimes used as an additive to ciders.

Other Species

Another species often planted in gardens, and sometimes along streets or in allées, is the European mountain ash, also called the rowan tree or quickbeam, *Sorbus aucuparia* L., and its various cultivars. This tree, which has naturalized through North America and even in Alaska, has composite leaves that turn yellow to red-orange in autumn. Its round red fruits are not edible raw. The showy mountain ash, *Sorbus decora* (Sarg.) Schneid., is named for its large bright red fruit, like small apples, which mature in the early fall. It is native to moist valleys and slopes in the northeastern part of North America, in Canada and as far south as Connecticut and west to Iowa.

THE SHOWY RED FRUIT OF THE MOUNTAIN ASH, REMAINS ON THE TREE INTO EARLY WINTER, PROVIDING FOOD FOR BIRDS. THE SPECIES NAME AUCUPARIA, WHICH MEANS "TO CATCH BIRDS," REFERS TO A CUSTOM OF SMEARING STICKY FRUIT ONTO BRANCHES TRAPPING BIRDS THAT LANDED ON THEM.

THE BRANCH

Fruit

Leaf

YOUR SERVICE TREE LEAF

PLACE COLLECTED : _____

DATE COLLECTED : _____

COLLECTOR'S NAME : _____

NOTES : _____

_____

_____

OTHER SOUVENIRS FROM YOUR WALKS

You can complete your herbarium by collecting in the following pages other leaves, flowers, or fruits gleaned from your walks.

PLACE COLLECTED : _____

DATE COLLECTED : _____

COLLECTOR'S NAME : _____

NOTES : _____

_____

_____

PLACE COLLECTED : _____

DATE COLLECTED : _____

COLLECTOR'S NAME : _____

NOTES : _____

_____

_____

PLACE COLLECTED :
DATE COLLECTED :
COLLECTOR'S NAME :
NOTES :

PLACE COLLECTED : _____

DATE COLLECTED : _____

COLLECTOR'S NAME : _____

NOTES : _____

_____

_____

PLACE COLLECTED :

DATE COLLECTED :

COLLECTOR'S NAME :

NOTES :

PLACE COLLECTED : _____

DATE COLLECTED : _____

COLLECTOR'S NAME : _____

NOTES : _____

_____

_____

PLACE COLLECTED : _____

DATE COLLECTED : _____

COLLECTOR'S NAME : _____

NOTES : _____

_____

_____

PLACE COLLECTED : _____

DATE COLLECTED : _____

COLLECTOR'S NAME : _____

NOTES : _____

_____

_____

PLACE COLLECTED :

DATE COLLECTED :

COLLECTOR'S NAME :

NOTES :

PLACE COLLECTED : _____

DATE COLLECTED : _____

COLLECTOR'S NAME : _____

NOTES : _____

_____

_____

PLACE COLLECTED :

DATE COLLECTED :

COLLECTOR'S NAME :

NOTES :

PLACE COLLECTED : _____

DATE COLLECTED : _____

COLLECTOR'S NAME : _____

NOTES : _____

_____

_____

Authors of the names of cited plants

The term "author" is used for the botanist who writes and publishes the first description of an otherwise unknown plant and gives it its scientific name.

Ait.: William Aiton (1731–1793)

Benth.: George Bentham (1800–1884)

Burck.: William Burck (1848–1910)

Carr.: Elie Abel Carrière (1818–1896)

C. A. Mey.: Carl Anton von Meyer (1795–1855)

Chaix.: Dominique Chaix (1730–1799)

Crantz: Heinrich Johann Nepomuk von Crantz (1722–1797)

Desf.: René Louiche Desfontaines (1776–1856)

DC.: Augustin Pyramus De Candolle (1778–1841)

Dode: Louis-Albert Dode (1875–1943)

Durazz.: Antonio Durazzini (published in 1772)

Ehrh.: Jakob Friedrich Ehrhart (1742–1795)

Franch.: Adrien-René Franchet (1834–1900)

Franco: Joao Manuel Antonio Paes do Amaral Franco (1921–)

Gaertn.: Joseph Gaertner (1732–1791)

G. Don: George Don (1798–1856)

Guinier: Philibert Guinier (1876–1962)

Hance: Henry Fletcher Hance (1827–1886)

Hemsl.: William Botting Hemsley (1843–1924)

K. Koch: Karl Heinrich Emil (Ludwig) Koch (1809–1879)

Koidz.: Gen'ichi Koidzumi (1883–1953)

L.: Carl von Linnaeus (1707–1778)

Lam.: Jean-Baptiste de Monet, chevalier de Lamarck (1744–1829)

Liebl.: Franz Kaspar Lieblein (1744–1810)

Loisel.: Jean-Louis-Autuste Loiseleur-Des-Longchamps (1744–1849)

Marsh.: Humphry Marshall (1722–1801)

Mill.: Phillip Miller (1691–1771)

Moench: Conrad Moench (1744–1805)

Münchh.: Otto von Münchhausen (1716–1774)

Née: Luis Née (published in 1789 and 1794)

Oliv.: Daniel Oliver (1830–1916)

Pers.: Christaan Hendrik Persoon (1761–1836)

Roth: Albrecht Wilhelm Roth (1757–1834)

Salisb.: Richard Anthony Salisbury (1761–1829)

Sarg.: Charles Sprague Sargent (1841–1927)

Scop.: Giovanni Antonio Scopoli (1723–1788)

Seub.: Moritz August Seubert (1818–1878)

Sieb. & Zucc.: Philipp Franz von Siebold (1796–1866) and Joseph Gerhard Zuccarini (1797–1848)

Skottsb.: Carl Johan Fredrik Skottsberg (1880–1963)

Smith: John Smith (1798–1888)

Spach: Edouard Spach (1801–1879)

Steud.: Ernst Gottlieb von Steudel (1783–1856)

Ten.: Michele Tenore (1780–1861)

Thunb.: Carl Pehr (Petter) Thunberg (1743–1828)

Walt.: Thomas Walter (1740–1789)

Willd.: Carl Ludwig Willdenow (1765–1812)

Index of common names

Birch 44

Black alder 40

Box elder 130

Catalpa 28

Caucasian wingnut 146

Chinese scholar tree 150

English elm 124

English oak 108

English walnut 142

European ash 134

European beech 60

European chestnut 52

Gray poplar 88

Holm oak 104

Hornbeam 48

Horse chestnut 24

Laurel 64

Linden 120

Lombardy poplar 84

London plane 80

Mediterranean hackberry 56

Mimosa 138

Montpellier maple 16

Mountain ash 116

Olive 32

Paulownia 36

Planetree maple 20

Scarlet oak 100

Service tree 154

St. Lucie cherry 96

Sweet cherry 92

Sweet gum 68

Tulip poplar 72

White mulberry 76

White willow 112

INDEX OF BOTANICAL NAMES

Acer monspessulanum L. 16

Acer negundo L. 130

Acer pseudoplatanus L. 20

Aesculus hippocastanum L. 24

Albizzia julibrissin Durazz. 138

Alnus glutinosa (L.) Gaertn. 40

Betula pubescens Ehrh. 44

Carpinus betulus L. 48

Castanea sativa Mill. 52

Catalpa bignonioides Walt. 28

Celtis australis L. 56

Fagus sylvatica L. 60

Fraxinus excelsior L. 134

Juglans regia L. 142

Laurus nobilis L. 64

Liquidambar styraciflua L. 68

Liriodendron tulipifera L. 72

Morus alba L. 76

Olea europea L. 32

Paulownia tomentosa (Thunb.) Steud. 36

Platanus x acerifolia (Ait.) Willd. 80

Populus nigra 'Italica' 84

Populus x canescens (Ait.) Smith. 88

Prunus avium L. 92

Prunus mahaleb L. 96

Pterocarya fraxinifolia (Lam.) Spach. 146

Quercus coccinea Münchh. 100

Quercus ilex L. 104

Quercus robur L. 108

Salix alba L. 112

Sophora japonica L. 150

Sorbus domestica L. 154

Sorbus torminalis (L.) Crantz 116

Tilia cordata Mill. 120

Ulmus proceda Salisb. 124

GLOSSARY

ALTERNATE: Leaves are called alternate when they are positioned one by one at different heights on the same stem. (When they are positioned in twos at the same height, they are referred to as opposite.)

BRACT: A much-reduced leaf, particularly one of the small or scale-like leaves in a flower cluster or associated with the flowers.

CORYMB: A short and broad, more or less flat-topped, indeterminate inflorescence, the outer flowers opening first. Resembles an umbrella, though the peduncles do not part from the same point on the principal axis.

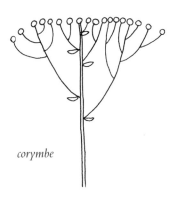

corymbe

CULTIVAR: Designates a plant obtained by selection, and cloned and cultivated to retain its characteristics.

CYME: A determinate inflorescence, with the central or terminal flower opening first. Made of a succession of ramifications, each ending with a single flower.

FASTIGIATE: Of a narrow, slender pyramidal shape.

HIBERNAL: Occurring in the winter.

LEAFLET: One of the ultimate units of a compound leaf.

LACINIATE: Slashed into narrow, pointed lobes.

LANCEOLATE: Lance-shaped, several times longer than broad and widest below the middle, and tapering to a point at both ends.

LENTICEL: Point on the outside of a branch or stem where cells are arranged to allow the exchange of gases between the air and internal tissues.

LIGNEOUS: Woody.

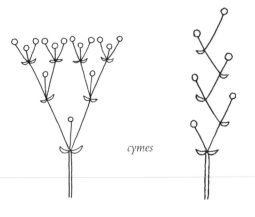

cymes

MARCESCENT: Said of leaves that wither on the branch, remaining there throughout the winter, and falling only with the arrival of new leaves in the spring.

PALMAT- LOBED: With three or more lobes radiating fanwise from a common basal point of attachment.

PANICLE: An indeterminate, branching inflorescence in which the flowers are arranged in a pyramidal shape on their stems.

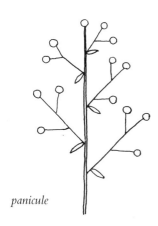

panicule

PETIOLATE: Having a petiole, or stalk, between a leaf, or fruit, and the branch it is attached to. A leaf that does not have this is called sessile.

PUBESCENT: Strictly, this means covered with soft, short, fine hairs; as commonly used, however, the term means hairy, bearing hairs, in a generalized sense, without reference to the type of hair.

SAMARA: A winged fruit, such as that of the maple (Acer), which holds one or two seeds, with a membranous blade in the shape of a wing.

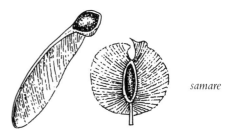

samare

SESSILE: The opposite of petiolate; possessing no stalk or connecting organ between the leaf, or fruit, and branch.

SILIQUA, SILIQUE: The two-carpeled fruit peculiar to the Cruciferae, in which two valves fall away, leaving a longitudinal central replum; the term is usually restricted to long fruits of this type, three or more times longer than wide.

silique

TOPIARY: The art of shaping certain plants into diverse forms by pruning or training.

VERTICILLATE: Arranged in whorls, or seemingly so.

BIBLIOGRAPHY

Bailey, Liberty Hyde. *How Plants Got Their Names*. New York: Dover, 1997.

Heinrich, Bernd. *The Trees in My Forest*. New York: Perennial, 1998.

Hortus Third: *A Concise Dictionary of Plants Cultivated in the United States and Canada*. 2 vols. New York: Barnes & Noble, 2000.

National Audubon Society Field Guide to North American Trees. New York: Alfred A. Knopff, 1980.

Peattie, Donald Culross. *A Natural History of Trees of Eastern and Central North America*. Rev. ed. New York: Houghton Mifflin, 1991.

Symonds, George W., and Stephen V. Chelminsky. *Tree Identification*. New York: William Morrow, 1973.

Thomas, P. A. *Trees: Their Natural History*. New York: Cambridge University Press, 2001.

Watts, May T. *Tree Finder: A Manual for the Identification of Trees by Their Leaves*. Rochester, N.Y.: Nature Study Guild, 1991.